Leo

The Ultimate Guide to an Amazing Zodiac Sign in Astrology

Your Free Gift (only available for a limited time)

Thanks for getting this book! If you want to learn more about various spirituality topics, then join Mari Silva's community and get a free guided meditation MP3 for awakening your third eye. This guided meditation mp3 is designed to open and strengthen ones third eye so you can experience a higher state of consciousness. Simply visit the link below the image to get started.

https://spiritualityspot.com/meditation

Contents

Introduction

Do you prefer being the center of attention or the queen bee in your group? Do you always feel on top of the world when someone gives you even the tiniest compliment? Do you care deeply about your family and friends? If you answered yes to these questions, you are probably a Leo! Go ahead and ask someone around you who has these traits; it is highly likely that they are a Leo, too.

Leos are born between July 23 to August 22 and are represented by a Lion as their sign. As a Leo, you might have heard people calling you warm, generous, and even vain at times. Leos are of an interesting zodiac sign, one that allows a perfect balance in their traits. While they are bright, chirpy, funny, and talented, they can also be stubborn and downright rude at times. Apart from this, Leos have many more layers to them. If you are a Leo or are concerned about one, you've come to the right place, because this book is all about the Leo and what makes them tick.

In this book, you will get a deeper understanding of the sign, which includes Leo's strengths, weaknesses, career paths, love and relationships, tendencies, and social behavior. The book will also give sound advice which will be useful in various settings such as parties, the office, or at home.

Whether you are a Leo or desire to know one, this book has got you covered. It explains everything about Leos – from birth to old age, rising signs, moons, suns, followed by explanations backing their tendencies, characteristics, and compatibilities.

This book provides you with the basic information needed, and then digs deeper, teaching you the lesser-known parts of this zodiac sign. It explores not only the traits and compatibilities of a Leo, but also the reasons behind them. In other words, it bridges the gap between a total 'newbie' book and an overly long dissertation and can be used by more experienced astrology buffs to brush up on the particulars of any given aspect of Leos.

Read on to learn more about this sign.

Chapter 1: An Introduction to Leo

Leos are born between July 22 and August 23 and are popularly known as the "Queens and Kings of the Zodiac." They are well known for their leadership qualities, creativity, confidence, and socializing skills. On the other hand, Leos are disposed to offensive degrees of arrogance due to their narcissistic and egotistical nature.

Before we delve into this sign's deeper aspects, it is necessary to understand the basic traits, characteristics, and information of this zodiac sign to strengthen the foundation of your knowledge.

Leos are mainly known for their fragile nature in terms of wanting and seeking attention. When they get the attention that they think they deserve, they seem to be the happiest creatures alive. It is difficult to decipher a Leo at first sight, or in one meeting. If you really want to know them, you must spend more time with them.

As a Leo, you are the star in your group and are always at the top of your game. Your caring and protective nature, especially toward your family, is praiseworthy and attractive. Your aura is bright, and you lighten up any room as soon as you enter, but you are always defamed for your arrogance, stubbornness, and constant need for attention and validation. As a Leo, you need your fair share of attention and always want to be in the spotlight.

Let's look at the elements, symbols, ruling planets, houses, colors, lucky numbers, gemstones, and most common traits of all zodiac signs to make a fair comparison with Leos.

Aries (March 21 to April 20)

Symbol: The Ram

Element: Fire

House: House of Self, which represents resourcefulness, beginnings, initiatives, and physical appearance.

Gemstone: Coral

Colors: Red

Lucky numbers: 1 and 9

Ruling planet: Mars

Most common traits: The most prominent trait of Aries is their competitive spirit and the need to achieve goals. Other than that, Aries are:

· Extremely creative and are blessed with an incredible imagination power

· A positive influence on others around them

· Full of enthusiasm and drive

· In need of constant attention and praise

· A bit self-centered and do not let people come too close

Taurus (April 21 to May 20)

Symbol: The Bull

Element: Earth

House: House of Value, which represents materialism, money, possessions, self-worth, cultivation, and substance.

Gemstone: Diamond

Colors: Pink, blue, and green

Lucky numbers: 2, 4, 6, 11, 20, 29, 37, 47, and 56

Ruling planet: Venus

Most common traits: The most prominent trait of Taurus is its ambitious nature. Other than that, the individuals bearing this sign:

- Possess a strong sense of intuition
- Are extremely dependable
- Always look for intimate and serious relationships
- Are extremely stubborn
- Have strong moral values

Gemini (May 21 to June 20)

Symbol: The Twins

Element: Air

House: House of Sharing, which represents generosity, distribution, achievements, siblings, communication, and development.

Gemstone: Emerald

Colors: Yellow and green

Lucky numbers: 3, 8, 12, and 23

Ruling planet: Mercury

Most common traits: The individuals bearing this sign are extremely social and possess a talent for making new friends easily. Other than that, they:

- Are super smart and energetic
- Have a bubbly nature and a positive aura
- Are funny and strategic
- Are known to be two-faced

· Have a need to over-analyze their environment

Cancer (June 21 to July 22)

Symbol: The Crab

Element: Water

House: House of Home and Family, which represents heritage, ancestry, roots, bond, comfort, neighborhood, security, and tidiness.

Gemstone: Pearl

Colors: White, orange, and silver

Lucky numbers: 2, 7, 11, 16, 20, and 25

Ruling planet: Moon

Most common traits: Individuals with this zodiac sign are extremely empathetic and are able to establish deep connections with others. Along with this, they:

> · Are known to be the caregiver
>
> · Possess a loving nature
>
> · Are partly governed by their emotions
>
> · Can be a bit difficult to deal with in intense situations
>
> · Can be a bit crabby due to recurring mood swings

Leo (July 23 to August 22)

Symbol: The Lion

Element: Fire

House: House of Pleasure, which represents entertainment, risk, enjoyment, romance, self-expression, and creativity.

Gemstone: Ruby

Colors: Orange, red, white, and gold

Lucky numbers: 1, 4, 6, 10, 13, 19, and 22

Ruling planet: The ruling planet of Leos is the Sun. Just like the Sun is the center of the solar system, Leos prefer to be the center of everyone's attention. Other planets revolve around the sun, which makes this for the same metaphor from another perspective.

Most common traits: Even though we will discuss Leo traits in depth later in the book, let's take a brief look right now at Leos' prominent traits:

· Leos want to be in the spotlight all the time. They want constant attention and validation from the people around them.

· They are warm, bright, and giving. Leos are known for their generosity and are often appreciated for their giving nature.

· They have expensive tastes. Leos can be materialistic and often indulge in expensive and luxurious objects, even if they cannot afford them.

· Leos are stubborn. They do not listen to most people and often resort to their own rules and decisions. Even if the other person is right, Leos will try their best to prove them wrong and win the argument anyhow.

· Leos are frontrunners. They have impeccable leadership skills and are ready to lead a team. Their personality and wise decision-making skills are appreciated by others, which makes it easier for people to follow their advice.

· They are brave and protective of their family and friends.

· Leos are passionate and romantic. When you are in love with a Leo, expect passion and heat in your relationship. Leos will expect the same in return. If they don't get it, be ready to console and comfort a snubbed Leo.

Virgo (August 23 to September 22)

Symbol: The Virgin

Element: Earth

House: House of Health, which represents strength, employment, vitality, healthcare, and skills.

Gemstone: Emerald

Colors: Brown, beige, yellow, orange, green, and navy

Lucky numbers: 5, 14, 23, 32, 41, and 50

Ruling planet: Mercury

Most common traits: Virgos need to help people around them, which makes them extremely dependable. They are:

- Super practical and hardworking

- Usually trying their best to keep people around them happy

- Resourceful and intelligent

- Believed to be obsessive perfectionists

- Despised for their criticizing nature

Libra (September 23 to October 22)

Symbol: The Scales

Element: Air

House: House of Balance, which represents marriage, partnership, business agreements, contracts, and equilibrium.

Gemstone: Diamond

Colors: Pastels, especially blue and green

Lucky numbers: 6,15, 24, 33, 42, 51, and 60

Ruling planet: Venus

Most common traits: This sign is extremely social and can make friends easily. Other than that, the individuals of this zodiac sign are:

- Full of wit, morals, and manners
- Extremely charming
- People pleasers
- Known to be great problem solvers
- Codependent

Scorpio (October 23 to November 22)

Symbol: The Scorpion

Element: Water

House: House of Transformation, which represents rejuvenation, birth and death cycles, resources, finances, karma, and self-transformation.

Gemstone: Coral

Colors: Dark red, scarlet, and rust

Lucky numbers: 9, 18, 27, 36, 45, 54, 63, 72, 81, and 90

Ruling planet: Mars

Most common traits: Scorpios are known for their ambitious nature and super-serious attitude towards work and their career. They are:

- Serious about relationships and can dive in too deep
- Extremely trustworthy
- Super-curious and in love with mysteries
- Controlling and hard to figure out
- Often suspicious about everything, which makes them paranoid

Sagittarius (November 23 to December 21)

Symbol: The Archer

Element: Fire

House: House of Philosophy, which represents culture, expansion, law, ethics, travel, and foreign affairs.

Gemstone: Yellow Sapphire

Colors: Purple, red, pink, and violet

Lucky numbers: 1, 4, 8, 10, 13, 17, 19, 22, and 26

Ruling planet: Jupiter

Most common traits: People bearing this sign are probably the most curious of all. They possess a thirst for knowledge and information. Other than that, they:

- Are hardworking

- Are always exploring new pursuits

- Possess incredible storytelling skills

- Are believed to be know-it-alls

- Often talk over others

Capricorn (December 22 to January 19)

Symbol: The Goat

Element: Earth

House: House of Enterprise, which represents career, society, government, motivation, authority, and advantage.

Gemstone: Blue Sapphire

Colors: Dark brown and black

Lucky numbers: 1, 4, 8, 10, 13, 17, 19, and 22

Ruling planet: Saturn

Most common traits: Capricorns are ambitious and put their career over anything else. Other than that, they:

- Bear a drive and unending passion for their work and achieving milestones

- Are known to take initiatives

- Form excellent leaders

- Have a slight need to control everything

- Do not believe in "me" time and work hard endlessly, which explains their stone-cold demeanor toward others

Aquarius (January 20 to February 19)

Symbol: The Water Bearer

Element: Air

House: House of Blessings, which represents effort, friends, groups, communities, belongings, volunteering, associations, love, and wealth.

Gemstone: Blue Sapphire

Colors: Turquoise, blue, green, and gray

Lucky numbers: 4, 8, 13, 17, 22, and 26

Ruling planet: Saturn

Most common traits: This sign loves their share of independence and wants freedom in every aspect of their life. Other than that, they:

- Have a unique personality that helps them stand apart from the crowd

- Are always looking for ways to change the world

- Are creative thinkers

- Often have controversial opinions in debates and conversations

- Feel the need to push their "unique" perspective in any matter

Pisces (February 20 to March 20)

Symbol: The Fishes

Element: Water

House: House of Sacrifice, which represents retreating, seclusion, refuge, intuition, luck, healing, peacefulness, and completion.

Gemstone: Yellow Sapphire

Colors: Sea green, violet, purple, and lilac

Lucky numbers: 3, 7, 12, 16, 21, 25, and 30

Ruling planet: Jupiter

Most common traits: Probably the kindest individuals of all signs, Pisceans are dreamy and passionate. Along with this, they:

- Are able to establish deeper connections with people
- Are extremely creative and positive
- Come up with new and imaginative ideas
- Are often lost in daydreams and are absent-minded
- Can get easily overwhelmed

Famous Leos

In this section, we will learn about a few famous Leos and their defining or most prominent Leo traits.

1. Barack Obama

This personality ranks number one on the list. An ideal leader, motivational speaker, and a compassionate human being, Barack Obama is probably the most significant Leo in the world's history. Born on August 4, 1961, Barack Obama is popularly known as a former U.S. President. Naturally, due to his leadership qualities, Obama tends to steal the spotlight in any setting. His speeches can be moving, bold, and clever. He is intelligent and possesses the ability to make a crowd follow him. Along with this, he is curious, possesses great communication skills, and can motivate a huge crowd merely by his presence.

Defining Leo Trait: He is a born leader. His charm is addictive, and people respect his opinion as a leader. We all know about the changes he made in the United States during his presidency and leadership.

2. Arnold Schwarzenegger

Schwarzenegger is another popular personality in the world of acting and fitness. He was born on July 30th, 1947 and has motivated many young adults to partake in their fitness journey and achieve their goals in this direction. Arnold is known to be kind, generous, and warm, which comes from the Sun sign of Leos. As witnessed in the past, Arnold is not able to take criticism easily and hates being ignored. He is a creative being and wants to show it to the world. His world revolves around drama, luxury, movies, and theatre, which is a prominent Leo trait in him. If you give him love, he will return an equal or greater amount of love to you. He often likes to be the center of attention.

Defining Leo Trait: He feels frustrated and discouraged when he cannot prove his worth. He will work hard to make a point and stand true to his word.

3. Bill Clinton

Another U.S. president with a strong and significant presence in world history, Bill Clinton is a Leo with strong traits of this sign. Born on August 19th, 1946, Clinton is another Leo that has proven his leadership skills as a Leo. While he did prove his leadership qualities in the professional and political world, his personal life was also dictated by his prominent Leo traits. He was known to be a womanizer with irresistible charm, if not looks. Women were smitten by his charisma and personality. His spouse was ready to let pass many of the negative traits that most Leos possess, which explains the strong bond between them. Lastly, when Clinton was in power, he had a motivational aura around him. The knack for drama in most Leos explains the controversy that surrounded the president.

Defining Leo Trait: As a Leo, Bill Clinton has proven his leadership qualities along with being a charismatic person and a strong personality, right from his younger days.

4. Napoleon

Born on August 15th, 1769, Napoleon Bonaparte was well known in the world for his military skills and for seizing the French emperor's title. As a Leo, he wanted his fair share of the spotlight. Even though this phenomenon was not literally named in the olden days, Napoleon always managed to be in the center and commanded others with authority. He was a brave fighter and leader in the military.

Defining Leo Trait: His bravery, the need to be the ruler, and leadership skills are apparent Leo traits.

5. J. K. Rowling

Famously known for her *Harry Potter* books and movie series, this author was born on July 31st, 1965. Her strong and charismatic personality captures the room as soon as she enters. She is also believed to be warm, kind-hearted, and generous, which are the Sun sign's indicators. Her generous trait is proven by the fact that she donated a major amount of her earnings to charity, which led to the removal of her name from the list of billionaires in Forbes. But she has recently been in the news for her new book and infamous "trans" comments, which explains Leos's penchant for controversial or dramatic gimmicks.

Defining Leo Trait: Her most prominent Leo trait is creativity. Her flair for writing and imagination skills are powerful, which aligns with some Leos. Also, her generosity is another powerful Leo trait.

6. Madonna

Born on August 16th, 1958, Madonna has been a popular figure since her youth. She is known for her confidence, singing talent, and exotic beauty. Madonna has always loved to be the center of attention and continues enjoying her fame and limelight. Her Leo traits are so centered that she can be deemed the epitome of the zodiac sign. Also, she can work on multiple projects at a time, which is a lesser-known Leo trait. She has been the center of many controversies and has somehow always managed to be in the spotlight.

Defining Leo Trait: Her charm, personality, and talent are some of the most apparent and positive Leo traits. The need to be the center of attention is her major Leo trait.

"Placing" a Leo

Even though Leo behaves the same in most settings, you can still notice subtle differences in their behavior due to a change of surroundings.

Leo at Home

While a Leo at work or in any other public setting is at the top of their game, they want to be in their own cocoon at the end of the day to release stress and take some "me" time. A Leo at home is more relaxed as they take time in their space to unwind and contemplate. In fact, when work and socializing become too extreme for Leos, they will often disappear and stay at home for a couple of days until they have their energy back. They want time off from the chaos of the world. Home is where they take time to recharge and return stronger, but even at home, Leos can be found exploring new options and skills. Give them just a day to relax, and they will be doing something new.

Leo at Work

At work, Leos take charge of a project or any other follow-ups where leadership qualities are mandatory. They are driven, motivated, and put in a 100-percent effort to achieve their goals, but they make sure that they are validated for it. If any of your colleagues are a Leo, you will find them near the boss most of the time. They will also try to make their work more noticeable. They want their boss to praise and appreciate them. If they don't receive positive feedback, Leos will sulk and even throw tantrums. If you are a Leo, you might notice yourself throwing a fit whenever you receive constructive criticism in an office setting.

Leo at a Party

Leos at a party are the show stealers. Their irresistible charm and extroverted nature attract people to them. If you are a Leo and are alone at a party, you will immediately find company and make yourself comfortable. Leos have no problem or awkwardness when they meet new people. They are spontaneous and masters at building new relationships in a jiffy. At a party, you will find a Leo either dressed too extravagantly or at the center of the stage; Leos love attention and will often engage in such meager attempts to garner attention.

Leo Cusps

Individuals born on the edge of two zodiac signs belong to a "cusp". These individuals have a combination of traits relevant to both signs. At the same time, you can also expect these traits to clash, which results in the unique personalities of those on cusps.

There are two cusps for every zodiac sign. In the case of Leos, they form cusps with Cancer, which precedes the Leo sign, and Virgo, which follows the house of Leo. Within these cusps, you can expect individuals who are entirely different from each other because of the Sun's dominance. An individual belonging to each cusp will possess qualities depending on the Sun's direction and powerful stance.

Cancer-Leo Cusp (July 19ᵗʰ to July 25ᵗʰ)

If the sun falls toward the Cancer sign, the individual will be too expressive, social, and a complete extrovert. Basically, the individuals born on this cusp are introverts who are on their way to becoming extroverts. They are also blessed with creative skills and generous nature. Sharing and receiving gifts will be routine for these individuals.

But if the Sun is on Leo's side, the individual feels vulnerable from the inside and possesses a lot of insecurities; it is very easy to hurt such individuals. People in this cusp can be at the top of their game one day and feeling sad and depressed the next. The sudden change in their mood results from the trait combination of both signs.

They behave like children and are stubborn. Even if they are hurt and feel insecure inside, they will not show it. Instead, they will mask it with a playful spirit. People born on this cusp are creative, courageous, loving, generous, and often self-absorbed, but they seem to be emotionally blocked at times.

Leo-Virgo Cusp (August 19ᵗʰ to August 25ᵗʰ)

If the sun takes Leo's side within this cusp, the individual will turn out to be a perfectionist. They will have an air of creative freedom and the need to express themselves. But if the Sun takes the Virgo's side, the individual is more expressive. A combination of these traits will form a person who is a perfectionist with a creative and playful flair.

People belonging to this cusp are always excited about beginning a new journey, especially if it is going back to school to begin a new term after a long summer break. An interesting aspect of this cusp is that people from both signs possess different egos. Virgos serve others while Leos expect others to serve them, which brings an interesting imbalance to this cusp. They will readily serve you, but with a flair of pride, almost with a portrayal of obligation. While they still behave like divas (which is a prominent trait in Leos), they will also arrange and fulfill their tasks on time, as most Virgos do. While this cusp is still a perfect choice for an actor or a celebrity in the entertainment industry, the Virgo side of this cusp is more apt to be a director.

Some Fun Facts about Leos

While learning their basic traits, elements, and other foundational information is necessary, you should also know a few fun facts about this sign.

- Leos love drama. They can be seen in or anywhere near a dramatic situation. Truth be told, Leos in high school would form a Drama Kids Club as their clique. Also, due to their fondness for drama, their ideal location would be Hollywood, California.

- Leos are believed to be addicted to shopping. Even if they are, or are about to be, broke, they will find a way to shop and acquire the things they like. Leos are known to be stubborn, so they will get what they want at any cost. Since shopping is an addiction, their desires often revolve around new clothes, shoes, and other luxury items.

- Leos will prefer a spiced pumpkin latte in Starbucks.

- An exotic phrase that suits Leos would be *la douleur exquise*, a French phrase that translates to "the pain of unrequited love," which describes their need and passion in relationships and love life.

- If they were to choose or assign a Harry Potter house in the zodiac, all Leos would most likely fit in Gryffindor.

- Given their need to be a star and in the spotlight, they would prefer a clothing item that is sparkly or anything that grabs attention. The glamor and pizzazz that comes from clothing items often enthrall them.

If you are a Leo, most of these fun facts will be relatable. As an exercise, think about other fun facts that relate to other categories with your traits. Consider categories like music, movies, books, seasons, food items, etc., and note them down.

Chapter 2: Strengths andWeaknesses of a Leo

After acquiring some basic information on the traits and other aspects of the sign, we will hop on to this sign's strengths and weaknesses.

Strengths or Positive Traits of Leos

Among the several positive traits of Leos, these stand out the most:

1. They are Warm, Bright, and Bring Love to People in Their Lives

Leos love and are loved by the people in their lives. They possess a bright and warm personality, often a sign of their ruling planet, the Sun. They love their family and friends unconditionally and bring peace and happiness to their lives. They are highly dependable, which attracts people. To top that, Leos are kind, compassionate, and polite, which makes them seem brighter.

A Leo will make sure that their family and friends are comfortable. Their hospitable nature is always welcoming. Whenever Leos meet someone, they immediately make them feel at home. But do not take advantage of their kindness, as they will easily pounce and take revenge without remorse.

2. They are Charismatic

Wherever they go, Leos take the lead stance and seem like the most important person in the room. Their personality, presence, and character collectively make Leos charismatic. Due to this charm, Leos can attract whoever they want, eventually making them stay for a prolonged period. A person's charm is often dictated by their positive traits, which explains Leos's charismatic personality. They are loyal, brave, good looking, and confident enough to personify charisma.

Along with this, they are also blessed with a great sense of humor. Their wit and jokes help them get where they want to go or fulfill tasks with ease. The charismatic personality of Leos is so magnetic that it is often compared to a moth attracted to a flame. Leos attract people and keep them entertained. Besides this, Leos possess power and are driven by ambition, which adds to their charm and powerful personality.

3. They are Social and Can Easily Build Relationships with People They Have Just Met

Leos have no trouble approaching strangers at parties or opening a conversation with people they have just met. Whether it's chit-chat with the staff at the convenience store or meeting a professional in a formal setting, Leos have it easy. They'll say "yes" when you propose to go out and don't have that "I just want to stay home" attitude that other signs have by default. You can call them extroverts who make others feel comfortable. They are highly likely to interact with people they find interesting or who share similar traits.

If you are Leo, you have nothing to worry about in a social gathering with strangers. You will easily befriend others and make yourself comfortable in any setting. If you are not a Leo, you will likely be approached by one. Leos just love to be around people. They cannot be alone and always look for opportunities to go out and socialize. Their extroverted nature triggers them to throw parties, social events, or small informal gatherings like weekend dinners to meet people.

4. They are Born Leaders

If you need anyone to lead a group project in your school or office or make important decisions as the leader of any pack, you can always turn to a Leo. They are reliable and take charge of any situation. They are quick on their feet and can decide easily, helping you navigate urgent situations that require spontaneity. Decision-making ability is needed in most leaders and is thoroughly fulfilled by Leos. As a Leo, your aura is regal, and you instantly inspire people to follow you. Even though you like being the center of attention, you work hard to earn it; it is not merely handed out to you, which is another reason why you want to take charge and lead the group. Leos also have an intuition that pleases the crowd which is why they are often in command and motivate their followers.

Consider the trait of being social in most Leos. They not only want to throw parties and meet people, but they also want to be in charge of the celebrations. Leos like being the host and leader in any event. They love to take charge of any formal or informal situation. Whether it's a political agenda, a national leader, a CEO of a company, or a host of a party, you can always rely on Leos to take the lead and make informed decisions. They never quit and work hard to accomplish their goals.

5. Leos are Highly Protective of Their Loved Ones

Leos guard their family, friends, and other precious relationships as much as they can. Their brave nature helps them tackle any obstacles and make sure that their loved ones are safe and at peace. They will go to any length to keep their relationships intact. They value their friends and family too much and will fight until their last breath to protect them and their relationship. If there is even a slight chance of the relationship being in trouble, they will try their best to fix it. Leos are extremely passionate. They give and want passionate love, to a point where it can get intoxicating.

Leos are known for their bravery and confidence, which enhances their protective trait. Since the Fire symbol guards Leos, they are passionate and put in all their energy to protect what they love. Leos' bravery trait is related to their protective nature and the willingness to perform risky activities. Leos are not easily intimidated by fearful circumstances and will take risks. Leos rarely say no and are most excited about activities that most people refuse to undertake. From going on dangerous hikes to investing money in a business, Leos do not fear risks. They are extremely adventurous.

6. Leos Forgive Easily and are Honest

No matter how much or how deeply they are hurt, Leos forgive easily and will give another chance to the people who have wronged them. Be it breakups, marriage, friendships, or casual relationships, they want to keep the people in their life, but for them to forgive others, they want an apology, and a sincere one. They don't hold grudges, which keeps them cheerful and happy most of the time. This positive trait of Leos lets them keep precious relationships intact.

Leos are probably one of the most honest signs in the zodiac. They stick to their word and pay all debts. When it comes to keeping promises, you can always rely on this sign. They are honorable and do what they say, but if they feel like they can't do it, they will say so to keep you from building false expectations; this saves both parties time and helps them move on. Their honesty is another reason they form good leaders and can lead a team to success.

7. Leos are Creative and Entertaining

They possess creativity and the perception to see things differently, which keeps their creative juices flowing. They are often seen trying out new hobbies and activities. If you have a Leo in your inner circle, you may notice that they are always up to something. Their passion for adventure and exploration is never-ending; it makes them joyous company with whom you like to spend time.

Equally, Leos have a great sense of humor that keeps the people around them entertained. Leos are not only entertaining but can also stay entertained themselves. Their constant need to do something and try new activities keeps them busy and enhances their skill set.

Weaknesses or Challenging Traits of Leos

Having gone through their strengths, let's now discuss weaknesses and challenging traits of Leos that could cause trouble in their lives.

1. Leos are Impulsive

At times, Leo can be quite impulsive. While taking immediate action without thinking twice is useful in some circumstances, it can also lead to a lot of problems. Let's take an example given earlier – investing in a business. It is a huge risk that needs concrete assumptions and demands calculated steps. You cannot simply jump to a decision. Even though Leos make informed decisions, this trait's spontaneity can also result in a major downfall due to unforeseen circumstances.

But when an opportunity comes knocking on their door, they will usually think twice before making a decision, which saves them from trouble. Their impulsive nature only kicks in when they get an idea and want to implement it. They just cannot wait to see an idea of their own taking shape, which results in impulsive decisions. When they are handed something they think twice, but they are quick to take the risk when they come up with their own plan.

2. They Can be a Bit Controlling

This weakness of Leos can lead to a failed relationship. Sadly enough, Leos do this unknowingly. Until they realize their controlling behavior, it is often too late. When this trait overshadows others, they could end up losing their partners. Many people break up with their Leo partners, ending relationships that lasted more than a decade.

For Leos, it is important to realize the nature of their controlling behavior and work at it. Failing to do so can result in incompatible relationships which eventually result in breakups or divorces. Their controlling behavior is also a reason for their stubborn nature because they feel they are right all the time; they believe it gives them the authority to control their partners and family. If this trait is strong in any Leo, they might repel people or even lose them forever.

3. Leos are Often Stubborn and Defensive

They are not ready to listen to others. When they desire something, they will go to great lengths to achieve it. It is helpful in occasional situations, such as achieving your career goals or working hard to buy a luxury car, but in situations where Leos should step back and listen to others, such as a topic of discussion in a social gathering, they often agree to disagree. Often, this stubborn attitude comes across as arrogance, unbeknownst to the Leo.

Also, when they are not allowed to have certain things, they don't listen and try hard to get them anyway, by any means. For example, a diabetic Leo will find a way to eat that chocolate bar that they craved. When someone says that they are not allowed to do something or that they are wrong, they will fight back to prove otherwise. Their defensive nature can be problematic. This nature of arguing and defending until they turn blue in the face is not appreciated by other signs, which is one of the few reasons for being repelled by a Leo. It doesn't matter whether they are right or wrong; if Leos think that they are right, they will do anything to prove their point.

4. Leos are a Bit Egoistical

Leos are probably the most egotistical among the zodiac signs, which can often be problematic. For the Leo, their large egos can be a major problem. They cannot handle criticism well and are easily offended. Even when they face constructive criticism, they can take it too seriously.

Their egos also pave the path to their selfishness. Leos feel that they deserve everything and more. They often put their needs in front of others, which makes them appear selfish and even greedy. Even though they realize this act is selfish, they hardly care and are unwilling to compromise. Due to their intelligence, they always feel they are above everyone else, which also explains their need to be in the spotlight. The hard part is, they manage to gain it somehow. The sense of entitlement is combined with their ability to take advantage of all opportunities thrown at them, feeding their ego even more. Their egos also make them believe that the world revolves around them.

5. They Cannot Deal with Their Insecurities

Leos are well aware of their insecurities and can be easily and deeply saddened when someone targets their insecurity, becoming even more insecure. In other words, their egos can be deemed their biggest insecurity. Since Leos have this urge to be perfect in the way they look, perform tasks, and every other aspect of their lives, any grievances against or pointing out of their insecurities can be too hard for them to handle. If it continues for a long period, they might even break. In a way, targeting their insecurity means pointing out their imperfections, which could also steal their spotlight. No Leo likes or wants that.

They want to be respected and praised all the time. If not, it could take a major toll on their self-esteem. Even if you don't mean it, they will take things personally and keep thinking about it time and again.

6. They Need Constant Validation

Leos need attention and constant validation. They make a show of not caring about others' opinions, but deep down, they need attention and love. A prolonged absence of validation can make them childish until they get enough attention. They feel the need for approval from others, even from people they have just met. When they work hard for something and do not get the praise they deserve, Leos can become too angry and even desperate to get their work noticed. Their usual thoughts are, "I deserve to be praised for something I achieved in less time than others," or "Why hasn't anyone noticed my hard work yet?"

This trait of seeking attention can drive them to show off and boast about their achievements, which is an attempt to come across as acceptable. They try hard to show what they are and want others to perceive them in this way, but their pride will never let them admit that they need constant validation; this trait is toxic and needs to be worked on for them to come across as humble and grounded. It is not easy, but with practice, it will come to them.

7. They are Unable to Bear Losses

Leos can be deemed hopeless romantics. They do need attention, but they are ready to give equal attention. But a minor inconvenience, insult, or loss in relationships can leave a deep scar in their hearts. In cases such as breakups and divorces, they not only get hurt but are also not able to bear the loss. In intense situations, this could lead to a major downfall and chaos in a Leo's life.

8. They Can be Too Materialistic

Leos are attracted to expensive objects and indulge in luxury. They tend to over-shop, and it is difficult for them to stop. If they like something, they will try their best to own it, no matter how expensive it is. To some degree, they will also judge people who are unable to afford or give them expensive objects.

How to Navigate Leo Weaknesses

If you are a Leo, possessing the weaknesses mentioned above is natural. Knowing about them is half the battle won, but you should also focus on navigating these to improve your life.

1. Set Long-Term Goals

Leos are impulsive and will take risks to see their idea to take shape in reality, but at times, this spontaneity can lead to failure. To combat this situation, a Leo should set some long-term goals. These might help a Leo to make more focused decisions and fulfill their goals with ease. Even though this approach takes time, it is a sure-shot way to achieve success.

So, how can a Leo set long-term goals? The first step is to define them. Ask yourself relevant questions like, "What do you truly desire?" or "Where can you see yourself in the next five years?" These questions will help you narrow down realistic milestones. Make sure that they are relevant, realistic, and achievable. If your goals are not achievable, there is no pointing in writing them down. To make them more plausible, cut them down into smaller goals or steps that will eventually lead you to the bigger picture. So, design your goals accordingly. Last, do not give up. If your ultimate goal is to buy your dream house, work hard toward it, and make it happen. Your smaller goals will be to save money and conduct research for the best properties in your locality. As a Leo, you will naturally have the drive to work hard and fulfill your goals.

2. Focus on Your Actions Instead

When a Leo finds themselves in a dramatic setting (which is quite often), they will likely reply with a snazzy comment or even swear at the other person. This tendency should be controlled and avoided. If you truly want to answer them in an impactful way, show them with your actions. If your boss bashes you for not reaching the goal sooner, work harder to achieve more than anyone in your office in the next quarter instead of answering back defensively. Ease up on the drama and divert your attention and focus toward achieving your goals instead of adding to the drama. As they say, "Focus your attention on turning lemons into lemonade instead of throwing them at others."

If your impulsive nature wants you to reply with harsh words, count to three before you say something. Even though it sounds clichéd, it does work. It will save you from saying something that you'd later regret. Try the "Big Gulp" action, where you signal yourself and make yourself more attentive. Also, take it one step at a time. Do not burn yourself out to achieve far-reached goals. Take it slowly and keep going at a steady pace. Consistency and patience are key to fulfilling your goals.

3. Try to Put Others' Needs Before Your Own

As a Leo, your selfishness might seem more apparent at times because you have obviously put your needs ahead of others.' It makes you come across as selfish, needy, and greedy. Individuals who know about this negative trait of Leos often try to take advantage of this, especially in a work setting, so it is necessary for you to navigate this negative trait and focus on others. Even though it is fair to consider your needs too, focusing too much on yourself will make you selfish and put you in a negative light. To navigate selfishness and put the needs of others before you, you must first acknowledge this behavior. It is believed that the more selfish people are, the less they realize the decree of their selfishness. So, reflect on your behavior and ask whether you are selfish or not.

Next, reflect on and realize what others are going through. For instance, if a grocery store clerk is rude to you, it could just mean that they are upset or having a bad day. At times, it is not what it looks like on the surface. Try to assume the best of the other person. Instead of thinking, "It's me against the world," change your mindset to "We should conquer our goals together." If your needs are still important, take what you really want and cannot do without. While you are doing that, make sure that you are not causing an inconvenience to others.

4. Prevent Arrogance

Leos are known to be arrogant and often look down on others. Even though they don't mean it, their regal aura and pompousness make them look arrogant. Sadly, Leos don't realize their pompousness and arrogance as they believe it to be self-confidence, which is perceived otherwise by most signs. This arrogance can even affect a Leo's personal relationships and career. Before it's too late, every Leo should learn to control this behavior.

The first step to combat arrogance is self-realization. Once you realize that you are arrogant, not self-confident, it will be an eye-opener. Increase self-awareness and try to perceive your behavior through others' perspectives. For this self-realization to occur, look for signs in your behavior. A cocky attitude, constant interruption, playing the blame game, and giving unnecessary or unsolicited advice are all signs of arrogance. Treating everyone around you as a competitor or the constant use of condescending words or phrases add to the arrogance factor.

Once you achieve this realization, you have won half the battle. Next, try to be compassionate to others and yourself. Don't take yourself too seriously and try to laugh at yourself. It shows humility and modesty. Treat yourself and others with kindness. Accept mistakes and try to learn from them. Don't try too hard to hide them. Lastly, enjoy your own company and do something that makes you happy and calm. Even though it will take time, consistent practice will help you combat arrogance. Since this is one of Leos's biggest weaknesses, overcoming or learning to navigate it will help you clear the blockage you previously had to succeed in life.

5. Stop Yourself from Buying Items That You Don't Need

Most Leos feel the urge to indulge in luxury and buy expensive objects, even if they cannot afford them. Since they want to be appreciated for their expensive taste, they will buy an item, even if it means emptying their savings. One simple way to prevent this is to put a stop to shopping urges. To do this, you must first acknowledge the fact that your attachment to materials is toxic and irrelevant. Attaching yourself to materials sets up a self-perpetuating cycle in life. The more you buy, the more you will want. It is why many people are resorting to the concept of minimalism, which implies that you must live as simply and minimally as possible, with only the objects that you need and not everything that you think you want. This practice has proven to bring inner peace and joy to people who have followed it for many years.

To control your urge, the first step is to put your needs in front of your wants. Before you decide to buy something impulsively, ask yourself whether you truly need it or not. If it's just a want and not a need, hold off on the purchase. Think about where you can put the same money for better use. Invest it somewhere or add it to your savings. Another way to stop impulse buying is to avoid going to the mall or shopping area entirely. Once you are near such an area, you will automatically be compelled to buy. So, to avoid impulsive buying, avoid going to the mall in the first place. If your friends ask you to hang out at the mall, avoid it at all costs. Yes, it will be difficult for you to resist, but you must learn the value of putting your needs in front of your wants.

Another trick is to freeze your credit card. If you don't have a credit card, never consider getting one. Cancel your credit card or freeze it until you learn to control impulsive buying.

While Leos are blessed with more positive traits, their small weaknesses can be navigated easily to bring their best personality forward. Even though they are stubborn, they are often regarded as the most generous, warm, and intelligent individuals in a room. Once they manage to navigate their weaknesses, they can easily achieve their goals and succeed in life.

Chapter 3: The Leo Child

In this chapter, we will talk about Leo children and the traits they express. You will also learn how Leos interact with other kids and what they can do to improve their relationship with other children.

Leo as a Child

Leo kids are usually generous and warm. They are full of energy and radiate positive vibes. They are often enthusiastic about their life experiences and endure every moment with happiness. Even though they look confident and tough from the outside, it is highly likely that they are vulnerable or even scared on the inside. They possess a touch of vanity, which hasn't developed fully. They look confident, but if you mess with them, it could hurt them deeply. In extreme cases, it could even destroy their self-esteem.

If you are a parent to a Leo kid, you may have to reflect on your tone when disciplining your child. Harsh or mean words can lower a Leo kid's confidence. It is then difficult for Leo kids to get back on track. So, maintain composure and train or discipline your kid in the right manner. Every Leo kid is on a constant hunt for approval and appreciation. Whether it's their parents, teachers, friends, or even guests at home, Leo kids will try their best to glean a word or two of praise. They are not shy and will enthusiastically perform a nursery rhyme or dance to hear a few claps from guests.

From a young age, Leo kids will look in the mirror, dress up, and try to gain everyone's attention around them. When they receive enough praise and appreciation, they will work harder to gain more attention; this is why they usually turn out to be successful, even if there is an ulterior motive attached. The confidence and skill set from a young age is another reason Leos have excellent leadership skills. Since the Lion represents Leos, they are blessed with natural leadership skills.

Leos are so talented and skilled that they might attract opportunities from a very young age. They are skilled enough to be actors in plays or even TV commercials. If they get selected to the football team, it's no surprise either. Leo kids will never shy away from the prospects of becoming popular and will make the most of all opportunities. Even if they don't do well initially, they will develop their skill set on the way and will ultimately excel.

Besides this, Leo kids are known for their honesty and loyalty. They will never lie, even if they will end up in trouble. As a parent of a Leo kid, you should reward them for their honesty; it will inspire them to be honest in the future. Leo kids are also known for their firm morals. Rewarding Leo kids for their honesty and morals are more important than praising them for their sense of style and looks. Otherwise, they will grow up paying more attention to the way they look instead of the way they behave.

Leo kids will make you laugh. Since all Leos have an ingrained sense of humor, they are likely to crack you up. They are likely to be the leader of their group. Since they are bossy, they might be arrogant with other kids. Teach your child the importance of giving a chance to others. Make sure that they learn to give up arrogance. One way to handle this situation is to enroll them in scouting camps. These camps teach kids to be leaders, be humble, and to put their best skills to use to progress in life. Given Leos's talent and creative skills, scouting camps are the best way to mold their personality and character from a young age.

Leo Kids at Home

Leos at home are the same – chirpy and enthusiastic. You will always find them exploring or investigating new areas of their house. They will either show their creative flair by coloring on the walls or stay busy spreading their Lego set all across the floor. Basically, you will find a Leo kid up to something unusual.

They are the naughtiest but also the funniest among their siblings. Even if their parents don't admit it, Leo kids are their most favorite. If they are learning to ride a bike, they will keep trying until they learn perfectly. Failure is not an option for them; they will fail multiple times but still get up and keep at it until they achieve their goal. For Leo kids, quitting is better than accepting defeat, which changes somewhat when they mature. To build their confidence, help them accept defeat; teach them the importance of making mistakes, and learning from them. Teach them not to give up but also not to put too much emphasis on winning. Even if you don't teach them the definition of winning, this sign is already born with it.

Leos at home are often seen busy in various activities, most of which are set up by their parents to teach them new skills. As a parent of a Leo child, find their creative outlet, and set time aside for them to practice at home, usually after school. It can be painting, origami, cooking, or even board games that develop their memory. Building these skills at a young age is necessary, and since Leos are already blessed with creativity, intelligence, and curiosity, it is easier for you to convince them to follow their creative outlet.

Leo kids might also force their parents to get a pet. They love animals and are natural caregivers. Since Leos are full of passion and have a lot of love to offer, you can expect this trait to be a part of their natural personality. Another reason Leo kids like pets is that they are always ready for snuggles. When Leos don't get attention for long, they can always resort to their pet, who is ready to shower their owners with immense love.

Leo Kids at School

Leo kids at school will often hover around their teachers to hear words of appreciation for their finished homework or a drawing they made in art class. If they don't get the attention, they will make a fuss about it and even throw tantrums to gain their teacher's attention. They excel at studies and are often top of the class. Whether it's an art class, drama club, or the sports team, Leo kids are often seen excelling at everything they participate in. They also inspire their friends and classmates to perform well. If a class has two Leo kids, they are most likely to compete. It begins with healthy competition initially but might soon turn into fights or even hatred. Since Leos want all the attention to themselves, they will hate sharing it with the other Leos in their class.

Leo kids are often the star of their young friend group. They lead the pack during classwork or when they decide to play a prank. They are influential and trigger their friends to take part in any activity. It is also because of their bossy attitude. Other kids follow the Leo kid and often want to be like them. If a friend in the group has misbehaved or played a prank on someone, the kids' parents will question the Leo kid first, who is most likely the group leader.

On the playground, you will see them running around energetically and playing cheerfully. They have an impressive physical strength, one that outruns the others. You'll often spot a Leo kid on a monkey bar or climbing up on other installations without fear. Their daring and fearless attitude inspires them to explore new areas and objects, even if it's playtime. Keep an eye on them as they could end up in dangerous situations easily.

Leo as a Parent

Leos make great parents and are often known to be generous, warm, kind, and wise. Like themselves, they want their children to enjoy every moment and make the most out of the opportunities thrown at them. Since Leos are extremely confident, they want their kids to portray their best self, too. They will make sure that their kids are the best dressed in the room and will not mind if their children show off a little. Leos will give enough playtime to their kids and let them have plenty of fun. They are not as restrictive as other parents of different signs and understand the need to have enough freedom. Since Leos are never used to being enclosed or on a shelf, they understand the importance of liberty and give their kids enough.

In exchange, the children of Leo parents usually turn out to be open-minded, creative, and confident. They might catch traits of vanity from their Leo parent, but it is often harmless. Leo parents push their kids to do their best and provide them with all resources they need. They are keen on developing their kids' artistic and performance skills and support their creativity.

There are some downsides, though. Leo parents are so focused on their kids that they often ignore their social life, which is very unhealthy for a Leo. At the same time, their kids can get too demanding due to being pampered. If you are a Leo parent and are facing such an issue, you can schedule playdates for your kids. It will give you time to socialize with your friends and build your kid's social and communication skills. Or you can appoint a babysitter.

After all, you are a Leo; you have the need to rule and be in control of your life. Even before you had your kid, you retained your interests and adjusted them to your busy schedule. By taking time off, you can also pay more attention to your kid, which will not seem like a duty after that. It's a great practice for you and your child's development. You will notice the difference in the long run. Even if you are not a parent, keep these points in mind for when you become one. Your child will thank you.

Leo Kids with Leo Parents

While you already learned about Leos as kids and as parents separately, you might be curious to learn about Leo parents with Leo kids. This pairing is extremely interesting as both individuals need their own version of the spotlight. Both of you possess warm personalities with a bright and radiant aura. You enjoy each other's company and always try to learn a new skill together. As a Leo parent, you are mature enough to give up your share of the spotlight to make sure that your kid gets enough attention. You are attached to and in awe of your kid. Their skills, confidence, and generosity are something that you appreciate every day. Make sure that you praise your kid every day and guide them to become a better person.

Even though you both display tough demeanors, you are soft and vulnerable on the inside. Your Leo kids are even more easily hurt than you are. Try to protect your kids by showering praise and affection. It will help them forget about the incident and motivate them to focus on the positive side of life. Make sure that affection and praises are real, as Leo kids will have a sharp sense of detecting fakeness. Your affection and attention are needed to make your kid stronger.

When two Leos meet, differences are bound to arise. Once you and your Leo kid get into a fight, it is very difficult to arrive at a verdict. Neither of you will back off easily, which is the stubbornness trait of Leos. While you want the best for your kid, they will not appreciate your refusal to indulge them. In moments like these, it is your spouse who settles the quest, as neither of you will accept defeat. It is also likely that one of you will hurt the other's feelings. Even though you hate it, you don't like losing, especially when you are trying to fight for your kid's betterment.

What a Leo Kid Needs to Thrive and Feel Comfortable

As you learned, certain weaknesses in Leo kids need to be navigated for them to develop a positive personality and character. At the same time, certain positive traits should also be used in the right way to mold the skills of a Leo child. As a parent of a Leo, it is your job to do that from the onset.

Here are a few ways to do that:

1. Find a Way to Dispel Their Energy

Since Leo kids are extremely energetic, their parents should find ways to channel all that exhilarating energy in the right direction. For instance, enrolling them in a swimming class, gymnastics studio, or a football coaching club are some smart choices to put their energy to the best use. It will not only help them develop athletic skills but also enhance their socializing skills. If they are consistent and perform well, they can also take it up as a serious career choice, but before you enroll your Leo child in any class ask them their preference, as they would follow their passion more enthusiastically. It might turn out that they don't even like sports or such related agendas.

2. Be Patient with Your Leo Kid

Since Leo kids are stubborn, they must be handled with patience. Whether it's refusing to wear a certain outfit or being adamant about not finishing the vegetables on their plate, your Leo kid can be too stubborn and refuse to listen to you. It is difficult for a parent to get their way with a Leo kid, as they don't listen and only do what they want to. Due to their short temperament, they are also bound to throw tantrums when you don't listen to them. Even though this stubbornness trait can help them deal with bullies in school, it has a higher chance of affecting them negatively. Dealing with their stubbornness with patience is key to handling and diminishing it. Pair it with a little exasperation to handle it better.

As a parent of a Leo child, it is necessary for you to stay calm and be patient during intense situations. For example, if your kid is being stubborn about completing their homework, be patient, and think about dealing with this situation calmly instead of scolding them. To combat this situation, you can say, "Look at your friend, he is getting such good grades. Bet he does his homework every day. No wonder he is always top of the class." Since Leos want to be at the top, they will be driven to take the top spot for themselves. You will notice your Leo kid instantly turning to their homework.

3. Teach Them Moral Values

Sudden outbursts and throwing tantrums in public places are a common scene for most Leo kids. At some point, it becomes so normal that most parents get used to it, but it could affect their personality and personal life when they grow up. The best way to control this situation is to teach your Leo kid the importance of values and moral behavior. The importance of being gentle, calm, and composed should be repeated for your kids to grasp the entire concept. At the same time, you must behave similarly. Since kids copy their elders, it is highly likely that your child will copy you, too. If you are calm and can handle the situation calmly, your kid will reflect the same behavior as well. Lastly, pat their backs to calm them down. When throwing tantrums, your little monsters are full of rage and annoyance. Stroke their hair or pat their backs to make them calmer and soothe their anger.

They will also feel disappointed upon being rejected. They tend to think that they have to be perfect to be loved and respected. Teach your Leo kid that it is okay to be comfortable in your skin and achieving perfection is impossible. If they are not taught at an early age, they often burn themselves out to achieve all goals, even if it means sacrificing food, sleep, and inner peace. Most importantly, teach them these moral values in private, especially if they have made a mistake. If you point out their mistake in public and try to correct it in front of others, they will feel hurt, and it might even pierce their pride. If you hurt a Leo's pride, you are automatically added to their bad books.

4. Play Calming Music

Calming music offers therapeutic benefits to all living beings. Its soothing effect is equivalent to meditation, which relieves stress and improves concentration. It is a useful way to make your Leo kid calm down and maintain their composure. Kids' brains start developing at a tender age and playing calming music stimulates your kid's brain and enhances its functionality. Studies have proven the positive effect of calming music on brain development. Since Leos possess a liking for music and dance, playing music will keep them active, improve concentration, and enhance their skills. Not only calming music, but you can also play the music that your kid prefers. Whether it's a meditation tune, a pop song, or a lullaby, any tune will help in developing a Leo kid's brain. Since Leos are creative and have a fondness for music, dance, drama, and any other cultural mediums, they might even take it up as a career.

5. Set a Routine for Them

Make a bedtime routine a thing. Give your Leo child tasks to do before they go to sleep; this, of course, involves brushing their teeth and changing into nightclothes, but can also include other household chores such as taking the dishes to the kitchen or straightening their room. Make sure that the tasks you give them are not silly, and that they feel them to be important – after all, your Leo child feels like a king and needs to feel important and worthy of the tasks. The routine helps them unwind their energetic attitude and makes them more grounded. They also learn some organizational skills, along with the importance of being organized. And they learn the value of helping others and working as a team.

Your child is most likely to respond to this exercise and help you because Leo kids are generous, understanding, and full of energy. Also, by giving them bedtime chores, they feel needed. Slip in other silly tasks within the list of chores, too, such as picking up their clothes off the floor and putting their socks in the washing machine. If these tasks are on the list, they will do them relentlessly. To make it more effective, ask your kid to cross off a task once it is done. It will give them a feeling of accomplishment, which is what most Leos live for.

6. Make Sure That They are Brought Up in a Loving and Positive Environment

Leo kids need positive reinforcement and praise to stay happy and motivated. While you shouldn't spoil them with unnecessary praises, it is important to keep them on their feet – this is true with kids of any sign. Since their brains, character, and personality develop at a tender age, they should always be surrounded by positivity and love. If so, you will find your Leo kid responding more positively. They will always carry a bright aura, a smile on their face, and infectious energy that motivates other kids, too.

If the Leo child is a girl, you might find her to be too clingy. This behavior is often a result of fear to show emotional commitment, which often comes in the absence of healthy relationships. Once she gets even a bit of affection and love, she tries to cling to it and doesn't let go easily. To correct this, make your household a loving environment. Show her that affection and love are normal and that she'll always be loved. At the same time, teach her the sense of loving others and giving it back.

As you learned, Leo kids are supremely talented, curious, generous, and warm beings. As a typical trait of a Leo, they need their spotlight at school, at home, and on the playground. They will try their best to garner attention and affection from their parents, teachers, friends, and guests. If molded in the right way, their personality oozes charm as they grow up, but they can be too stubborn and do not yield easily. Also, they are fierce and loyal. If you break a Leo kid's trust by lying, they will turn a cold shoulder toward you, even if you are a parent. Even though they will forgive you easily and give you a second chance, they will hardly forget it and may bring it up the next time you repeat the mistake. Lastly, Leo kids are extremely confident, which will help them achieve their goals with no hassle. Pair that up with their creative skills, and you will have a leader in front of you.

Chapter 4: Leo in Love

We have now arrived at one of the most awaited parts of this book, which covers relationships and Leos in love.

Leos are passionate and fiery when it comes to love. Yes, we are talking about a mad, passionate, and intoxicating love that we often see in movies and read in books. They are not only excellent lovers in life but are also sensual in bed, but if left alone, Leos are brave enough to walk alone without any hesitation. They either love hard, or they don't – there's no in-between. If they love passionately, they expect the same in return. If you have a Leo for a partner, they will go to any lengths to prove their love and keep you safe. They expect the same in return, however; one wrong move and they are easily turned off. So, make sure that you are honest and able to reciprocate a Leo's love.

Compatibility with Other Signs

In this section, we will draw out a compatibility chart for the other zodiac signs and determine the most compatible sign for Leos.

Leo and Libra: While Leos are known for their competitive spirit, they would rather share the spirit with Libras instead of competing with them, and both traits will enjoy their spotlights. Not being competitive about it with Libras helps Leos attract them as potential long-term partners. If they enjoy being in each other's company and let their partner enjoy their part of success and spotlight, and even encourage them and participate in the celebration, all will be well.

Leo and Scorpio: Leos get more spotlight compared to Scorpios, which is not really an issue for the latter. In fact, they participate in the celebration and appreciate Leos for their achievements, but Scorpios do want their share of power, especially in a relationship with a Leo. If they don't get it, they could end up in a huge fight that could even destroy the relationship. Since Scorpios are known to choose and fight their battles wisely, there is a balance between these signs until one gets too hungry for power.

Leo and Sagittarius: Probably one of the most compatible pairings of signs, Leos and Sagittarius form a great couple and live their lives peacefully. There is hardly any drama in their daily lives. They create and achieve goals together. They enjoy each other's company so much that they divert their attention to accomplishing tasks that will help them reach their goal sooner. They talk less and do more. Along with this, they always have busy schedules and are rarely found at home because of their seriousness toward their career and goals, in which both signs support each other at every step. The fun-loving and adventurous nature of Leos is often well complemented by a Sagittarius.

Leo and Capricorn: These two signs are less likely to be attracted to each other, but when they are, they form a strong couple that is concerned about their reputation. This couple will work hard to establish their reputation and make sure that others see them as they want them to. While the need to be respected is stronger in Leos, Capricorns have a strong work ethic and are goal-oriented, which makes them shine in their professional peers' eyes. If they set their minds to it, this couple can win the world and achieve all their goals.

Leo and Aquarius: Aquarians and Leos have a higher chance of being sexually attracted to each other; this attraction often leads them to indulge in a non-vanilla relationship that is often casual. It is hard for these two signs to get involved in a serious relationship because they hardly have anything in common, but if they set their minds to it and work harder to make it happen, they can emerge as a strong couple. If you are a Leo and want to get into a serious long-term relationship with an Aquarius, you should make every effort to know the person inside and out. Since you do not have many similarities, knowing your partner will help you sustain the relationship.

Leo and Pisces: When compared to Leos, Pisceans are needy and want more attention, especially in relationships. Their need to be loved, nurtured, and understood falls on their partner. If a Leo does not fulfill the need, the relationship could end sooner. Also, Leos are stronger and more confident compared to Pisceans. The latter can easily crumble under serious circumstances and lack confidence; this is when Leos bring the balance with their high confidence and strength. If a Leo truly loves their Piscean partner, they will go to any lengths to protect their partner and nurture the relationship. In fact, in a Piscean and Leo relationship, the entire responsibility of handling and stabilizing the bond falls on the Leo. Also, the mutual understanding between both signs keeps the boat sailing, but if a Leo feels tired of being too strong over a prolonged period, the relationship could break.

Leo and Aries: Another great compatibility bond, Leo and Aries are known to be good friends and partners. Both these signs love spending time with the other. Even if they do nothing together, they feel comfortable in each other's presence. One peculiar trait that this couple possesses is that they have zealous and jealousy-inducing social tendencies. Deep down, they don't want their friend or partner to spend time with others and have the tendency to get jealous easily, but with understanding and trust, they can easily get over the jealousy factor.

Leo and Taurus: Since Leos possess the need for attention, a Taurus can get easily agitated. They don't appreciate the need to always getting validated, which triggers a Taurus; this could make them jealous and cause bigger problems in their relationship. A Taurus barely knows that they deserve to relax and take time off their busy schedules, whereas a Leo will always feel like being on edge.

Leo and Gemini: While none of these signs excel at "adulting", they can stay busy having fun all the time, which will alleviate the stress of responsibility. They know that they are in charge of their lives, bills, and survival, but they may fail to face this reality and cover this denial phase by playing together too much. They enjoy each other's company and rarely need a third person to have fun. They make each other laugh and only take responsibility when something falls out of order.

Leo and Cancer: Like a Taurus, a Cancer does not enjoy Leo's attention-seeking trait. They feel that their need for attention and validation is insincere, shallow, and inauthentic. While they do not want the spotlight on themselves, they also do not appreciate Leos always wanting to be in the spotlight, but once a Cancer gets to know a Leo, they can tolerate or let go of this need and flow with it easily. While they do not appreciate it, it doesn't have to bother them either. Since both these signs are massively different from each other, they hold the potential to complement and support each other.

Leo and Virgo: The relationship between both these signs is more mature compared to other pairings. They are open and ready to accept each other's strengths and weaknesses, resulting in an extremely mature and happy relationship. These signs are quite compatible and help each other at every step of the relationship. A Virgo doesn't mind a Leo taking the spotlight, which is appreciated by the Leo. This pairing proves that real balance can exist in relationships.

Leo and Leo: A Leo dating a Leo can be volatile at times as both need to be in the spotlight. Unless the partners are mature or are ready to let go of this weakness, the relationship can be too toxic; this is particularly witnessed in Leos who are in the same profession as their partner. A Leo couple who are both doctors or architects can often end up in a never-ending argument due to their need to be the star and their stubborn attitude. Leos who want to be in a serious and long-lasting relationship must find a balance and make it work somehow. It can only be achieved if one or both partners agree to take a step back when things are heated. But since Leos feel the need to be validated, they often give compliments and pay full attention to each other.

The teen Leo's first-time relationships, or acting on an attraction, can be interesting. Teenagers are often quite immature and don't know what to say or how to behave in certain circumstances, and this can be a major backlash for Leo teens exploring their first relationships. Leos need attention and want to be validated. It is a trait that is heightened in their teenage years when they are transitioning into adults. Their call for attention will be extremely loud in this phase, which could make things worse, but since they are attracting people their age, this can go both ways.

In an entirely opposite scenario, teenagers or other Zodiac signs might ignore Leo teens' attention-seeking trait. They may not understand the constant need for attention. Most teenagers of all signs will show similar behavior, which will make first relationships either too easy or too hard.

Most teen Leos are charming, good looking, have a great sense of style, and attract others to them. If you are a Leo and like someone, ascertain whether they have a problem with your garnering attention or not. If you belong to another zodiac sign and are attracted to a teen Leo, you will find them in big groups and difficult to approach.

So, what approach should teen Leos take to explore their first relationship? The wisest advice is to take your time. You must work on your pride (which comes from the Lion) as it could throw you off balance and make you rigid. Your teenage years are where your character and personality grow rapidly, so you must take enough time to build yourself before you find love. Since teen relationships for Leos might fail due to a lack of understanding, immaturity, and the inability to find a balance between both partners, it is wiser to wait for a few years.

First Relationships and Falling in Love

While falling in love and maintaining a relationship is easy for Leos, it can be very difficult for them to find an ideal partner. Even though the Lions are ready to go all-in, it takes time for them to find a partner who aligns with their needs. Even if they find someone, being in a long-term relationship is harder, the reasons for which will be explained in the next section.

Leos are open to dating and will take every shot at it. They are open-minded and do not hurry to judge a person without interacting with them properly. They savor every phase of dating – from feeling the butterflies to taking it to bed, and don't mind doing it all over again. For them, even dating is like an adventure; the more you explore, the better you know.

They do build a set of expectations before going on dates. They want their dates to behave and turn out in a particular way. If not, it can be disappointing for Leos, and they might take some time before going on the next date. It is highly likely to happen, because it is difficult for Leos to find an ideal partner. Only the lucky few rarely struggle in the dating world. At the same time, they do not mind going back to past relationships and giving them another chance. As Leos are extremely forgiving, they expect a person to change and behave up to their expectations. If this happens, they also occasionally find true love with exes or past dates.

In the bedroom, Leos get steamy and wild. They are passionate lovers, even on their first date. Due to their adventurous nature, they might also suggest videotaping their experience, if the partner is comfortable with it; this also explains their fondness for dirty talk. If you want excitement in your first relationship or date, you can always count on a Leo. If you are Leo, you must find someone who is ready to jump on the crazy bandwagon with you. When it comes to sexual encounters, the partners of Leos are lucky as Leos don't tire of pleasuring their partners, but they expect the same in return. So, if you are up for it, you will have a long ride in the bedroom.

Leo in Marriage or Long-Term Relationships

In this section, you will learn about the obstacles that may occur in a Leo relationship and how their traits (which were briefly explained earlier) influence the relationship.

· You might not like your Leo partner garnering attention. If you are someone who likes attention too, the relationship could turn into a competition, which is unhealthy. On the other hand, if you don't like attention but don't like others seeking it, it could also cause trouble in a long-term relationship with a Leo.

· They will act childishly if you don't give them enough time. It could be difficult to keep your Leo partner satisfied when you are under a lot of stress.

· Their fiery temperament can be quite a handful at times. If you disagree with anything they say, their temper can be explosive, which can lead you into an endless pit of arguments. They will go to any length to prove their point and win the debate (even if they are wrong), which can be extremely frustrating.

· If you cannot afford expensive things and gifts, your Leo partner might lose respect for you. While this is not always the case, and they give enough time for development, constant failure can be too off-putting for them, which could end a long-term relationship.

A Quick Guide to Dating a Leo

If You are a Leo

Two Leos as a couple can either be very strong or quite disastrous. Since they both equally need attention and do not appreciate anyone else being in the spotlight, the other person might become insecure. But Leos know and understand the feeling of being in the spotlight which gives them some leeway around each other, but this comes only with balance. If the partner is not mature enough or lacks understanding, it could lead to a breakup. So, before you date a Leo, talk to them about this. If they are not really into horoscopes, they will initially not believe in this foresight and immediately jump into a serious relationship. You are then responsible for carrying it off smoothly.

If You are Another Zodiac Sign

Depending on your zodiac sign, you will either love or despise your partner, in which case you will break up with them soon. While Leos are cheerful, hard-working, and passionate, their constant need for attention will either be off-putting for you or will hardly matter to you. If you are a Sagittarius, you have a high compatibility chance with Leos as you are least bothered about fame and wanting attention. On your first date, you will notice your Leo date flirting with the bartender or server. It is unintentional and far from being intended to make you jealous. They are just trying to squeeze in their occasional need for attention. You and your date know that you are the one going home with them. Also, it is highly likely that your date will dress well. They will appreciate it if you do, too, but make sure to draw the line early, as overshadowing them can steal their spotlight, which they will hate.

Attracting and Dating a Leo Man

Leo men prefer to feel like a king and want to be treated as one, especially by their partners. To seduce a Leo man, divert all your attention to treating him like a king and make him feel important. Just like Leo women, Leo men are also attracted to drama, so make sure that you add enough drama elements in your narration and overall experience with him. If you really want him to like you, give him respect and compliment him every once in a while.

He likes to hear compliments about his looks, so slip in tiny compliments like, "I like how your lips crinkle when you smile," or "Your big eyes are distracting." Do not make the compliments too obvious. Keep it low key; Leo men appreciate that and might even shake to a tiny dance in their heads. Also, make sure that the compliments are genuine. You do not want to come across as fake; Leos are smart, and they will instantly peg your fake compliments. Don't merely say it for his sake; mean it. The best part is you won't have to dig deep for compliments. Leo men are gentle, compassionate, and kind, which are easily complemented traits.

If you give him this treatment and attention, a Leo man is bound to reciprocate similarly and shower you with equal love and care. Once you attract a Leo man, be ready to be showered with gifts and passionate love. If you truly love him, you must show patience and prove your worth to him. Leo men need the assurance that their partners are strong and capable of handling tough situations in relationships. If you succeed, a Leo man will love you endlessly and passionately. If you really like a Leo man, be prepared to face some struggles, as Leo men are constantly on the hunt which means you might face serious competition from other women.

Keep trying and seducing him the way he likes, and if you succeed, you will be rewarded for it with gifts, luxury, and royal treatment. At the same time, be happy always and do not complain. Leo men adore cheerful women who can match their energy. Show him that you have a knack for adventure and are ready to explore new places with him. Leo men will love that and be attracted to you instantly, but when the time comes, prepare yourself to endure the adventure. Simply saying and not doing it can be a major turn off for Leo men, which could also mean that you were lying just to impress him.

Lastly, Leo men want their partners to be conscientious of how they feel. If he loves someone deeply, he will not show it easily, but he is 100-percent devoted to this relationship and always considers himself as the hero in the relationship. He gives you assurance and keeps you grounded. He proves the phrase "everything will be alright," to be accurate and reliable.

Attracting and Dating a Leo Woman

Just like Leo men, Leo women, too, need constant attention, praise, and compliments. All women like compliments, but Leo women are particularly keen to hear comments on their looks and personality. But understanding Leo women can be too complex. There is a major mix of positive and negative traits, so much so that finding a middle ground is too difficult. While some men with other signs can easily put up with Leo women, others prefer to stay away, especially if they hate someone who constantly seeks attention. If you are among the latter, you might want to rethink your decision to date a Leo woman.

Also, while dating a Leo woman, you must shower her with gifts, luxury, and this goes without saying – lots and lots of attention. Basically, a Leo woman should be the center of your world. Unless you are madly in love with her, this is next to impossible. If you are ready, make a note of all her rules and follow them religiously. Failing to do so can trigger her easily, and she will leave without giving you a fair warning, but since Leos forgive easily, she might take you back after a sincere apology. Just make sure that this doesn't happen in the first place because Leo women are hurt easily, and it is very difficult for them to get over losses.

Jealousy is a prominent trait in Leo women. Once she senses another woman in your life or close to you (even if it is platonic), she will leave you without giving you a chance to explain. Be careful and clear about your relationships with other women. As you know, Leos are controlling, which is very evident in Leo women. They will not listen to their partners and will try to control them. If you date a Leo woman, she will most probably decide what you can wear, eat, and do. She'll rarely let you have your own way. She will dominate you, but you will create a liking for it and let her control you because you know that she wants the best for you.

To attract a Leo woman, you must make her feel that she is one of a kind. She enjoys luxury, so an expensive gift once in a while will make her happy. Along with expensive gifts, this sign also appreciates worthy deeds. Choose an expensive and chic restaurant for your first date, because for Leo women, first impressions matter. If you are rich, you have a better chance of being accepted as a partner; this is due to their liking luxury and expensive materials. If you have nothing to offer except pure feelings, you might not stand a chance.

She is passionate in bed but does not appreciate games and experiments. The more love and passion you show her, the more a Leo woman will reciprocate equally or with even more love in return. She will be instantly attracted to you if you prove your worth and come across as a strong and independent individual but show her that she can depend on you. Treat her like a queen, care for her, and love her passionately.

A Quick Guide on How to Navigate a Healthy Relationship

Some Useful Tips for the First Date

If applied on your first date, these tips are bound to impress your Leo date and take it one step ahead. Even though some of these tips were briefly covered in the earlier sections, this short guide will sum up and offer extra ways to impress your date effectively.

· Let them choose the location. If you are planning to go on a date with a Leo man or a Leo woman, let them choose the location for the first date. They will likely choose something extraordinary, bizarre, or out of place because of their knack for adventure. They also want you to explore new places with them, so go along with it. After all, going to a place they prefer is better than choosing a place they might not like, which is a risky move when trying to make a first impression.

· If they give you the choice of selecting a location, they will appreciate a place known for its peculiar setting, expensive food, or class. It can be an expensive restaurant or even a musical play, since Leos love drama. Take them to a fine diner or dainty restaurant after the musical or theatre play. Give their curious souls variety and choices to devour. By doing this, you are allowing their creative inner child to come out, and this effort of yours will stay imprinted on their mind for a long time. If you really want to impress them, seek something adventurous and completely off the wall like a river-rafting experience or a hot-air balloon ride. Since they are into exploration, they will love the idea.

· Go for the finer things. Leos like everything luxurious, classy, and expensive. If you are at a restaurant, order the finest wine and try something new to eat. They prefer an expensive taste and like those who show and possess a liking for the finer things. If you are meeting a Leo woman for a date, buy her exotic and beautiful flowers that match her classy taste.

· Reach for the check or, at least, convince them to split it (if they reach first). Even though Leos will take charge and insist on paying the bill, they will appreciate it when you make an effort.

· If you are in a club, they might ask you to dance with them; remember their need to be in the spotlight, and don't say no. They like energetic people and want you to join them. Even if you hate dancing, make an effort. It doesn't matter if you suck at it; it's the effort that counts.

· Compliment them in a conversation. As mentioned earlier, do not forget to give compliments. It will put you in their good books instantly, and they will develop a liking for you. If you show interest, they will also show an interest. Get a bit touchy, but not in a creepy way. Leos are seasonal flirts and don't mind occasional sensual touches. When you first meet them, give them a huge hug instead of a handshake. Touch their hand when you feel excited or while giving a compliment; this mainly works when you are on a date with a Leo man. With a woman, it could come across as creepy and uncomfortable, so act accordingly.

· Give them a lot of attention, especially if you are meeting them with other friends. If a Leo gets lost in a crowd and does not get attention, they might feel snubbed. When they try to steal the spotlight, give them attention, and make them feel important among other people. A Leo man or woman will remember that for a long time and appreciate your concern.

How to Navigate and Sustain a Long-Term Relationship

Even though attracting and dating a Leo man is difficult in the beginning, it can be extremely rewarding in the long run. Your Leo man does need attention and assurance initially, but once he gets it, he will protect you until his last breath. So, dedicate yourself 100 percent to this relationship.

Here are some effective ways to navigate and sustain a long-term Leo relationship:

· Give equal love and passion. Leos are warm and compassionate. When they give love, they want to receive an equal amount or more back. So, to sustain your relationship, love each other passionately.

· Leos are extremely loyal. Needless to say, cheating can ruin any relationship, but with Leos, it will leave a deep scar for a prolonged period. They will break up with you and feel deeply hurt and bruised as their loyalty was never reciprocated. So, stay loyal, which is key to every relationship.

· Go above and beyond with flattery. If your Leo husband looks dapper in the new suit, tell him that. If your Leo wife is rocking the new heels, tell her that you cannot wait to be beside her in bed. Build a foundation of flattery, and you will have a long-term relationship; more importantly, a passionate and happy relationship.

· Amp up the drama. If you find an opportunity to show or let your Leo partner experience any sort of drama, do it. Since Leos love tiny doses of drama now and then, this will keep them exhilarated and excited.

· Do not hold them back. Leos are born leaders and have a strong desire for authority. If they want to build a new business, let them; if they want to lead a group project in their company, encourage and support them. Holding them back will stifle them, which is the last thing they want.

· You might have to lower your guard and listen to them. Leos are controlling, stubborn, and don't listen to others. Unless you think that they are absolutely wrong, you must listen to what they say. Failing to do so could result in fights, which could also mean the end of the relationship. If certain fights seem to get out of hand, give them time to reflect on their thoughts, and cool down.

· Don't let past mistakes or encounters ruin your present. Leo men despise it when you bring up the past and throw it in their face. Being the practical beings they are, they would rather divert their attention to the present and solve it. While it is hard to get an apology from Leos, they will sincerely apologize when they realize their mistake, so keep away from fishing for apologies. Let them realize it on their own and act accordingly. At the same time, they also do not entertain any kind of passive-aggressive behavior. Consider it a complete no-no as it could ruin your relationship completely.

Leos in love are either too rewarding or completely disastrous. If you really like a Leo and want to reap the benefits out of your relationship, you will have to put in some effort and have a lot of patience in the beginning. If you manage to navigate your relationship in the said manner, you will emerge a strong couple.

Chapter 5: Leo at a Party and with Friends

Even though we already discussed the brief traits of a Leo at a party, we shall take a look at it in detail. In this chapter, we'll discuss Leos's ability to befriend others, Leos in a typical party scene, their behavior and interactive ability, and follow up with a look at the mechanics of fostering a Leo friendship.

The sign of Lion indicates the pride of Leos, which is also shown in their friendship. Compared to other signs, Leos take utter pride in their friendships and their ability to make new friends. They will go out of their way to prove their friendship and assert a positive disposition in this area. However, they might not like friends who take the spotlight and attract attention more than they do, so they carefully measure their stance and decide to move ahead accordingly. Someone who looks, dresses, or performs better than them can be a serious threat, and Leos would rather keep them away than fear the absence of attention.

Despite this feeling, if a Leo really likes a person and wants them to stay for a prolonged period, they will support them and try to get over the feeling of not being validated enough.

Leo Friendship Grid with the Other 11 Zodiacs

The friendship of Leos with other zodiac signs is quite interesting, especially with a few of them. Even though Leos are sociable and make friends easily, you can witness a peculiar platonic relationship with each sign.

Leo and Libra: The friendship radar of these two signs is strong. It is more about admiration. Both signs like and admire each other's qualities and are inspired by their respective positive traits. For instance, a Leo will always go to their Libra friend for book, music, and movie recommendations, given their impeccable taste in art. Their subtle charm and grace are captivating. Instead of being paranoid, Leos also admire Libras and prefer to learn a thing or two from them. On the other hand, Libras love the way Leos live. The glamor and pizzazz surrounding Leos is something that most Libras would also like to experience. Both signs are charming, but Libras are more subtle and do not shout it out loud.

Leos, on the other hand, don't hold back. They snap at waiters or growl at bartenders if they don't get the service they expect. Being the master of etiquette they are, a Libra friend might feel shy or even embarrassed in these situations. They cannot be as bold as Leos and would prefer to diffuse the situation in a calmer tone. Leos are annoyed by the indecisiveness of Libras. When they are on a shopping spree or in a restaurant, a Libra might take a lot of time to decide the clothes to buy or the food to eat, which is quite annoying for the impatient Leo. Their impulsive nature cannot wait and compels them to buy both. These two signs must let go of these minor differences to celebrate a beautiful friendship bond.

Leo and Scorpio: Both signs are passionate, which could result in an intense friendship. For Scorpios, the most attractive trait about Leos is their warmth and affectionate nature because Scorpios face frequent dark impulses which can be eliminated, or at least, avoided in the presence of bright Leos. Their vibrant nature cuts off all negativity, and Scorpios prefer to experience that once in a while. The friendship between these signs has numerous confusing moments. It is difficult for Scorpios to decipher their need for the spotlight, while on the other hand, Leos are always confused about the privacy factor of Scorpios.

Once both signs get into a fight or even a minor debate, both will fight until the other party agrees, which is nearly impossible in a friendship between a Leo and a Scorpio. As a Leo, you will fight until the other accepts defeat, which is also the case with your Scorpio friend. To avoid the chance of this ruining your friendship, the safest bet is to avoid getting into a fight in the first place. Surprisingly, this trait of Leos is what draws them to each other. Scorpios give Leos a heated and stimulating conversation, something they could even learn from. Even though both parties will hopefully agree to disagree, there is always some valuable take-away from these encounters.

Leo and Sagittarius: These two signs get along well, especially compared to other pairings. In fact, this pairing is probably the most popular and compatible. The sign of Sagittarius, which is the Archer, is extremely compatible with the Lion, the sign of Leos. They are represented by fire, which means that they are equally passionate and share a liking for adventure and exploration. Even though a Sagittarius prefers being alone, a Leo's social skills will drag them along in a crowd, which introduces a perfect balance. A Sagittarius will not mind being dragged. When these two signs plan to go on an adventure, it is usually one of their best times spent together. While any time spent together is valuable for these two signs, adventurous experiences always excel. It is also because both signs healthily challenge each other and bring out their daring sides. In other words, they bring out their best courageous selves and inspire each other to achieve their goals. When a Sagittarius and Leo become friends, nothing can stop them from achieving the things they want.

At the same time, they mold themselves to present their most acceptable selves in front of the world. They try to be what others want them to be, mainly to garner attention. However, when they are with each other, they can easily let the guard down and show their true selves. They bond not only over adventures and exciting trips but also over a warm cup of tea. They enjoy each other's presence and can stay for hours in comfortable silence.

Leo and Capricorn: As a Leo, even though you are the life of the party in most settings, others still admire the presence and authority of Capricorns in the same room. Instead of being intimidated by their presence, you also admire their personality. Capricorns want things their way and will make them happen at any cost. So, if you are the master of snapping at someone for attention, consider Capricorns to be above you. Due to this, there might be tiny tiffs in a friendship between a Leo and a Capricorn. If given charge, Capricorns could even beat your leadership skills.

However, to sustain a friendship between these two signs, it is wise to find a real balance and join hands to win together. For instance, the Leo can take center stage, and the Capricorn can back them up by being the backstage authority, which is more crucial in any event. Give them the backstage or behind the scenes, and they will happily hand the center stage to you. This pairing is one of the strongest. Tiny annoyances from both ends include a Capricorn's pessimism and negative outlook toward life and a Leo's ego and impatience. However, these are malleable, avoidable, and should not affect the friendship too badly.

Leo and Aquarius: For Leos, Aquarius is probably one of the most diametrically opposing or contradictory signs of all. However, since opposites attract, this forms an interesting friendship pair. A Leo's need for constant validation and affection differs from that of an Aquarius, who hardly cares about anyone's opinions and doesn't feel the need to be validated. While Leos are more warm, extroverted, and lively, Aquarians are more reserved and prefer to be on their own. Similarly, while Leos think with their heart and let their emotions get the best of them, Aquarians are more practical and think logically.

If there are so many differences between both signs, what makes the friendship so interesting? One reason is loyalty. As you already know, Leos are loyal and are known to be one of the most trustworthy signs. It is an attractive trait that draws others and keeps them in their lives. Just like Leos, Aquarians are also known for their loyalty, which brings both signs closer. Once you, a Leo, are friends with an Aquarius, you will never ditch each other for impromptu dates or other reasons. Also, Aquarians will never talk behind your back or share your secrets with others, which makes them a trustworthy friend. Instead of facing minor annoyances, you might face certain confusing situations. For instance, your Aquarian friend might always talk in abstractions or try to have nuanced conversations with you, which can be confusing. But your conversations might mainly include fashion, drama, or grooming products, subjects which are not their cup of tea.

Leo and Pisces: Pisces are usually shy, which makes you want to protect them. As a Leo, your protective trait is brought out, and it brightly shines when you are around a Piscean. Pisceans have fragile egos. To help combat this, Leos often give occasional compliments to Pisceans to lift their spirits. Sometimes, Leos also give them expensive and thoughtful presents. Due to these gestures, a Piscean friend values friendship with Leos and is intrigued enough to keep the bond for a long time.

At the same time, Pisceans return the gestures by having an open mind and always lending their ears to Leos. Pisceans tolerate the nagging of Leos and actively listen to them. They offer sympathy and even comfort them if need be. Pisces don't like to be tied down and are free-spirited; since Leos can be possessive of their objects and even relationships, it might seem imposing on Pisceans. They want to explore their options and meet new people, which Leos don't like or appreciate. At times, a Pisces friend drives Leos crazy because of their absent-minded nature. Since Leos prefer a little perfection, certain absent-minded habits such as wearing mismatched shoes or socks and forgetting their wallet at home can be annoying. But, again, it is something that can be ignored and overcome easily.

Leo and Aries: These two are represented by the Fire sign, which represents their warm and affectionate nature. These two signs are gentle with each other. Like Leos, Aries are passionate and enthusiastic about most things in life. Due to this, both signs are always up for an adventure, which can strengthen the foundation of their friendship. When both signs are together, everything is more upbeat and elevated. For instance, when a Leo shares a normal joke with an Aries, it is ten times funnier to them. Similarly, any mediocre dish will taste better if it is made by one of the two.

There are a few negative repercussions in this friendship, too. While Aries dislikes Leo's aversion to calculated decisions (Leos are usually spontaneous and impulsive but will be too timid to make a decision that is not theirs to begin with), Leo despises their brutal honesty. Also, gaining attention and being in power could create some issues. Leos like to be in the center, and Aries want their share of power. However, both these signs usually come to an agreement as they like each other's company and don't want to ruin it. They would rather have fun together than ruin it due to such petty differences.

Leo and Taurus: These two signs are extremely different – the way they think, dress, eat, and perceive life. However, Leo and Taurus do share some similarities. For instance, both signs love luxury. They are fond of everything expensive. Another similarity is loyalty. Both signs are extremely loyal and will hardly ever cheat on their partners, friends, or any circumstance in life. Thirdly, both signs need a lot of attention. The Taurus follows the Bull sign, which means that they could equally be stubborn. If they want to eat something that the Leos don't like, they'd still prefer it anyway. Also, since both signs need attention, they could compete for it time and again, but in a healthy way. It is extremely difficult for both signs to yield, which could grow grudges.

However, this is not the case with close friends. If a Taurus and Leo decide to be close friends, they would hardly worry about the other grabbing the spotlight. Both will be given equal and fair chances to hold their center without feeling snubbed. The secret is to look beyond each other's weaknesses and celebrate their strengths. As a Leo, if you are able to do it, you will have a strong Taurus friendship that has the potential of lasting a lifetime. Also, you can learn a thing or two from each other. For example, a Taurus can learn some fashion tips from a Leo, whereas a Leo can learn money-saving tips from the Taurus.

Leo and Gemini: Gemini are bubbly, high-spirited, and have an air of lightness around them. Despite their age, they seem eternally youthful. Most Leos possess a serious demeanor, which can be treated with the playful aura of a Gemini. In fact, Leos want to bring their inner child out but are unable to do it. A friendship with a Gemini can bring that out and fuel a Leo's childish spirit. With a Gemini, a Leo feels radiant and happy and forgets their worries and stresses for a brief period. Every moment with a Gemini is fun and filled with joy.

With a Gemini, you can get into food fights or play a prank in public places, but the Gemini will handle the situation or clean up the mess. Leos are too high-maintenance to clean up any mess, which is a minor annoyance for Geminis. However, since they enjoy their time together, a Gemini doesn't really mind. On the other hand, Leos appreciate and also despise their Gemini friend's urgent need to clean things up and make everything perfect. Also, Geminis are unable to focus on a particular aspect for a long period, which annoys most Leos. These tiny annoying details are not really a big issue and can be easily avoided, which both signs successfully do, and it results in a precious friendship between both these signs.

Leo and Cancer: Most Cancers are moody, which could pose a threat between both signs. Cancer usually broods or is in a bad mood over minor inconveniences, which really annoys a Leo because Leos are warm, bright, and chirpy most of the time. At the same time, it is difficult for a Cancer to comprehend the sunny mood of their Leo friend. However, they do try to learn and adapt. Even if they cannot do that, they mostly let it go. Cancers are loyal and protective, which is also true with Leos. These similarities attract both the signs to each other.

A Cancer friend is extremely caring and wants the best for their friends. As a Leo, you can expect your Cancer friend is cooking up and putting your favorite dishes on the table when you visit their house. They make sure that their friends are comfortable. Also, a Cancer friend will always compliment a Leo, which is another reason Leos prefer to stay with Cancers. It doesn't stop there; as a Leo, you give equal love and care. Like other pairings, you will have your minor annoyances and tiffs, but both signs understand that friendship is more important.

Leo and Leo: Friendship between two Leos is imperative in terms of disclosing their full potential, talent, and beauty. As a Leo, a fellow Leo will understand and truly comprehend your personality without you even trying to explain it. You, too, will appreciate and be impressed by the bundle of talent that your Leo friend possesses. Both of you will be able to fully understand each other and satisfy the needs of a Leo in friendship. You will be drawn to each other in the first meeting and might develop a strong rapport within the next few. Once you befriend a Leo, be ready for inside jokes, frequent hugs, and occasional compliments. In a way, it will be like looking in a mirror and trying to understand your alter ego.

However, there might be some downsides to this friendship pairing. Your strong egos and constant need to be in the spotlight will affect your friendship. As you know, Leos hate sharing attention, which can affect your developing friendship. You will feel that your problems are bigger than your Leo friend's; your friend might feel insecure about the attention you are fetching. If you want to develop a friendship that will last long, this selfishness and the need to be at the center must be avoided or eliminated. If you are capable of doing this, your friendship and bond will be rock solid and indestructible.

Leo and Virgo: Virgos are known to be fastidious, which can be a bit annoying for other signs. However, Leos love this particular Virgo trait and even want to learn a thing or two about it. After all, this Virgo friend of yours will make sure that you are dressed nicely with a perfect hairdo. Basically, a Virgo will never let a Leo be embarrassed due to bad dress sense (which is highly unlikely anyway), bad hair, or even with food stuck in their teeth. Since Leos are all about showbiz and looking good, they will love having a Virgo friend around. Above all, Virgos don't need the spotlight and don't mind Leos having it all, which forms a perfect balance.

Since Leos always return favors and give equal importance to others, they will never fail to complement their Virgo friends. They appreciate the intelligence and practicality of Virgos, which boosts their fragile egos and makes them look on the brighter side of life.

Even though it sounds perfect, there are some downsides to this friendship. Virgos are all about etiquette; they despise seeing Leos throwing a fit now and then. On the other hand, the neuroses of Virgos are enough to drive a Leo crazy. Again, just like other friendship pairings, try to let go of these tiny grievances as it could cost you a beautiful friendship.

How do Leos Behave at a Party or a Social Gathering?

Leos love parties and informal social gatherings. They not only get a chance to glam up but also garner a lot of attention. Such events are a great opportunity for Leos to make friends and meet new people, some of which can be useful contacts for the future. Parties are a place where Leos can unleash their true wild side and be crazy. They love to sing, dance, and enjoy every moment. Whether it's a round of "Never

Have I Ever" or mere board games, Leos are up for everything as long as it is fun.

Leos are well known for their ability to make friends and increase their circle. With friendship, their motto is "the more friends you have, the easier life is." Out of the contacts they build, they slowly choose people who could have the potential of turning into close and life-long friends. At times, they don't even have to choose; if it is meant to be, Leos will automatically grow fond of them and suggest ideas to spend time together.

Whenever Leos enter a social gathering, they imagine a red carpet being rolled out for them. They dress to impress, which automatically puts them in the spotlight. As soon as a Leo steps into a room, they are bound to turn a few heads. Not only because of the way they dress, but also due to their personality.

When Leos meet new people, they instantly connect with them, mainly because of their heightened confidence. Not everyone has the confidence to approach others and start a conversation out of the blue. They take command, not only the conversation but of the room, and rule until it's time to leave. Also, they usually will leave early, especially if they are not getting enough attention; if, on the other hand, they are, they might even stretch an all-nighter. Since they are easily bored and distracted, they might nudge their partners to indicate the "it's time to leave" signal. You will rarely find Leos in quiet night outs where there are merely a few people unless the night out includes only their best friends.

They also have a tendency to flirt with waiters and bartenders to get free drinks and complimentary desserts. If you are short on money and still want an extra glass of beer, you can rely on your Leo friend. They will use their charm to get what they want. Even if not for free stuff, Leos flirt to gain attention. It gives them occasional spasms of joy and is enough to make their night legendary.

According to the personality traits of Leos, they are best suited to a pool party. It's a perfect chill-out event for Leos where they can meet and socialize with a bunch of friends at the same time. Since this sign is always up for something extraordinary and outdoorsy, a pool party is the perfect setting for a warm summer afternoon. If you are a Leo, chances are you will invite even your frenemy to show your hospitality and skills as a host. In other words, you'd want to show off and make them jealous. Even though it sounds petty, Leos don't mind doing it repeatedly.

If Leos throw an indoor birthday party or host a dinner, they expect their guests to dress nice, but not nicer than them. Close friends and guests of host Leos know this and ensure that they are appropriately dressed for such events. Unless you are decked to the nines, you will fail to impress your Leo host. This sign tries to create events from the smallest moments in their life. Whether it's a housewarming, welcome party, or a farewell, they will ensure that there's a party or an event just around the corner. If that's the case, they will divert their attention and stay excited until the time arrives. They will already know what they are wearing and make sure that everything is arranged perfectly. After all, a Leo is known to be an amazing host, and so, everything has to fall in place.

How Leos Make Friends and How to Foster a Leo Friendship

As mentioned earlier, Leos possess the natural ability to make friends easily and socialize with no trouble. They have a lot of contacts and friends, and their network is huge. Their social skills are commendable. They can easily converse with a stranger, reply to texts, slide in DMs on Instagram, and make plans instantly. One moment they are talking to a person in the department store, and the next moment they are invited to Leo's happy hour. Leos just need to "click" with others, after which they are your friend or at least a contact on your phone.

While Leos do give 100% to maintain their friendship and keep their friends happy, they expect the same in return. Their chirpy and bright aura attract people, but it is difficult for others to maintain a long friendship with Leos. Only those who can tolerate stubbornness and don't care about the spotlight can be good friends with Leos. In other words, friendships with a Leo is not easy.

Due to this, they will have fewer friends, and this contradicts the fact that they can make friends easily and often have a large group completely. Here, we are talking about real friends, with whom Leos prefer to share their feelings, and the ones whom they consider family. These friends that stay will last long, probably for the rest of their lives. They stay because they are able to tell a Leo their best and worst. They made an attempt to know the Leo at a deeper level, which unraveled their true personality. Not everyone is able to do that with a Leo. If the Leo is not close to you, they will rarely share their feelings. If they do, feel honored. As a friend of a Leo, it is your duty to praise them and make them feel wanted constantly. If you give enough love and attention to your Leo friend, expect the same in return. Once Leos realize that their friendship will last long and cement this belief, they will make sure that their friends are happy and comfortable. Exchanging expensive gifts is usually an unspoken tradition, given the expensive tastes of Leos.

Another reason Leos are unable to keep and maintain all friendships for long is that they are difficult to pin down. They have planned all their time, and their social schedule is always tight. Even if someone wants to strengthen their friendship bond with Leos, they cannot find time for individual meetups. Your best shot would be to attract their attention in a social gathering or when you are in a group. If the first few attempts succeed, you have a better chance of entering the Leo's private group of friends. Having a Leo for a friend is valuable as they are not only the life of the party but will also go to any length to foster their friendship with their besties.

The Value of a Leo Friend

To befriend a Leo, you must show them your bold side. Leos love those who live fearlessly and out loud. Leos are brave and appreciate others who possess the same quality. Leos feel instantly attached to those who share the same traits and thoughts.

When a Leo approaches you to talk, they will make you feel comfortable. They are the major carriers of any conversation. To keep their attention and take the friendship to the next level, listen carefully. Even though they will not talk about anything personal or share their deepest secrets with you, they probably will spill some beans or even gossip about the happenings around them. They do love their dose of drama. Even if you don't like gossiping but want to be friends with a Leo, nod along and try to be an active part of the conversation.

It is also highly likely that a Leo will talk about some new place they want to check out or slide in a statement or two about their latest expensive purchase. If you want to be in Leos's good books, compliment them often; it is the cheat code to building a friendship or relationship bond with Leos. Give them compliments and make sure they get their dose of attention frequently. If you are easily annoyed by this habit, you must reconsider your desire to build a friendship with Leos as it is their natural trait.

Here are three reasons a Leo friendship is valuable:

1. A Forever Bond

If you manage to get close to a Leo and know all their life secrets, you have locked them in for life. Leos are master connectors. It is difficult for other signs to befriend them; however, once they share their inner secrets and feel close to you, this friendship is bound to last for the rest of their lives. In fact, Leos become a part of your family and treat you like one of their own.

2. They are Generous

If your best friend is a Leo, expect expensive presents on your doorstep occasionally. Leos are generous, giving, and kind. They always have a plan to surprise you with presents and plans out of the blue. It is always rewarding to be with a Leo. Not just with gifts; Leos are generous with other aspects of friendship too. If you face any trouble in life, Leos will try their best to help you overcome difficult situations. Whether it's financial, emotional, physical, or any other issue, Leos will ensure that you get out of it and help you as much as they can.

3. Life with Leo Friends is Exciting

Leo friends are always up to something. They have a plan devised for the next gathering or "hang-out". You will always find yourself in a new restaurant, exploring new places, or going on an outdoor adventure. They cannot stay in one place and will drag you along. If you are an introvert who likes staying indoors, being with a Leo will change your social life completely. You will meet new people often and find yourself in crowded parties or clubs. The strange part is, you will enjoy it and ask for more. Also, since Leos are the life of the party, you will also be perceived as an A-lister and conceded commensurate importance.

How to Sustain a Leo Friendship

Here are some ways to sustain a Leo friendship and maintain it for the long-term.

· If you are a Leo and want to befriend a Leo, you both must arrive at a mutual understanding to let them share the spotlight with you. As you know, Leo friendships can be difficult due to the fact that they despise sharing the limelight.

· Go on adventures. A nice way to hang out with your Leo friend and strengthen your friendship bond is to invite them on adventures. Forest hikes, amusement parks, wine tasting tours, etc., are some great ways to lure a Leo into spending time with you and explore new places at the same time.

· Let them take control. Leos love to be the boss, host, and leader of any formal and informal event. If you are okay with the choices and decisions of your Leo friend, let them plan the schedule while you just enjoy the ride. Being the perfectionists they are, you will never have a dull moment, so enjoy every bit of it. Even if you want to be in charge, Leos will somehow fight for their stance and never allow you to take control. To avoid such fights and keep the friendship flowing for long, simply give up and let them have their way.

· Never lie to them. Leos are honest, loyal, and true to their word. They will never lie to you and will expect the same in return. Failing to do so will make them paranoid about your friendship, and they will never trust you again. If there is something that you are afraid to tell your Leo friend, you may resort to lying. However, if your Leo friend finds out, it will cost you your precious friendship. It's safer to be honest. Leos are known to be forgiving and are ready to give second chances. Also, they will appreciate your honesty.

· Compliment them often. While they may not get enough compliments and attention from strangers (which they will hate), it is your duty to make your Leo friend feel wanted. By compliments, we are not talking about giving fake compliments that might make them overconfident and vain; give real compliments that will lift their spirits.

To sum up, a Leo friend is generous, giving, caring, warm, and the perfect host. They might demand their need for the spotlight and validation, but other than that, a Leo friend is extremely valuable. They will return equal affection and make you feel valued. Whenever you are in need of a friend, a Leo will stand close by you and try their best to pull you out of trouble. Along with this, they will be honest and loyal until their last breath.

Chapter 6: Leo at Work: Career Paths for Leos

This chapter talks about Leos' career paths and how they behave in a work setting.

Great Careers for the Leo

This is an interesting topic of discussion. As you know by now, Leos possess a range of distinct personality traits, which can make it difficult to place them in a particular spot. It also gives them a chance to consider different career paths tailored to their traits. Let's check out a few of these career options and why Leos should consider them.

1. Broadcasting

Since Leos are lively and confident, being a broadcaster is an excellent choice. This career option lets them take the spotlight and allows them to be heard. TV and radio broadcasting are two niches within this discipline. Depending on your preference, you can choose either of these. Leos enjoy talking and are blessed with excellent communication skills, which makes this option a great fit as a career. Whether it's TV or radio broadcasting, a Leo will own the spot and add more pizzazz to turn the broadcast into a success.

As a Leo, if you have parts of Sagittarius or Gemini in your horoscopes, you should definitely keep this career option on your list. A PR executive is another great career option for Leos. Rumor control, sending and maintaining press releases, and navigating crucial information are important tasks of a PR executive. If you are a shy Leo who likes their occasional share of attention, this role is apt for you. It not only lets you maintain a private life but also gives you a dose of public attention every once in a while. Other career options in this line are life coach, on-air host, and nutritionist.

2. Designer

Leos can be great designers due to their passion and creative skills. The best choice for a designing career can be graphic or fashion. It is an excellent career choice for Leos, especially if they have parts of Aquarius or Virgo in their horoscopes. They are good at creativity, but they are also known for putting themselves out in the market. While other signs do creative work and wait for others to notice them, Leos try to display their work and make it noticeable. Since the design discipline is highly competitive, Leos will try hard to navigate their way and be noticed.

You already know about Leo's love for clothing, fashion, and glamor, which is well-served in the fashion industry. They know how to dress well and try to dress others in the same way. Even the fashion industry is highly competitive, but Leos know how to make the most of all opportunities. They will find a unique way to display their work, market themselves, and excel in any discipline. They are not afraid of competition and will face it like a true Lion. The confidence of Leos will help them tremendously in any design discipline.

To get into graphic or fashion designing, you first need to build your creative skills. Try to strengthen your observational skills and perceive objects differently. If you are into fashion, research and find your niche. Take relevant courses or build your own design portfolio after some practice. Apply to design agencies or work as a freelancer.

The discipline of design doesn't need a degree, so if you are thinking of changing your career, it is never too late.

Coco Chanel, Yves Saint Laurent, and Michael Kors are some famous Leo fashion designers.

3. Actor

As you know, Leos love their share of drama. They prefer to be in and around anything dramatic and possess a flair for theatre. They love watching movies and theatre plays, which are also great ideas for first dates with Leos. Acting is a great career choice for this sign as it offers glamor, pizzazz, attention, and drama, all in one place. Also, the red carpet and spotlight are perfect for Leos. You will notice a ton of actors and actresses with this sign. If you possess a talent for singing or dancing, you can also become a musician, which gives an equal amount of center stage.

Other sub-niches within this discipline include theatre artists, theatrical agents, and stage directors. Even if they cannot act, they get to be a part of the acting profession, which is enough to garner the required attention. Also, Leos get to show their management and organizational skills with this job position. In this job, they interact with famous actors, casting agents, and other significant figures of the movie industry. Any other profession related to this career option, such as art direction, museum director, lighting design, and costume design is suitable for Leos. Sandra Bullock, Daniel Radcliffe, Jennifer Lopez, and Lisa Kudrow are a few famous Leo actors and actresses.

A modeling career is also an appropriate choice for Leos. They get to be in the spotlight (quite literally) all the time, and they garner the attention of all the people in the room. Besides this, they get to be a part of the glam world. Walking for designers and wearing exquisite outfits and makeup is the dream of most Leos. If they excel in what they do, Leos can easily make it to the top.

Those Leos who cannot make it to the top due to high competition can also pave their path by being social media influencers and endorsing products of big brands. As a social media influencer, you can get a lot of followers and be showered with validation, which is heaven for most Leos. Besides that, Leos are also known to be great marketers due to their ability to convince people; this helps them sell the products they endorse. The best part is, you get to keep products you endorse from various categories – makeup, cosmetics, electronics, clothes, etc.

4. Standup Comedian

Yes, Leos can be comedians too. Their youthful, playful, and charismatic nature is addictive. Also, Leos are naturally funny. They can crack a joke or two out of the blue. Leos are great entertainers, and, using their bubbly and confident nature, Leos can make great standup comedians. They also get their share of spotlight and attention, which, as you know, Leos love. As a Leo, if you have parts of Sagittarius or Gemini in your horoscope, you should definitely keep this career option on your list. This career will not only give you fame but is also extremely rewarding. Also, if you are very good at what you do, other opportunities will come knocking in no time.

Some famous Leo standup comedians are James Corden, Teddy Ray, Victor Pope Jr., and Drew Lynch.

How to become a standup comedian: The best way to start is through social media. Social media platforms like YouTube, Instagram, and Facebook have billions of users collectively, which is a wide audience to entertain. These platforms allow you to share clips of your standup comedy. Before you begin recording and sharing your clips, write funny narrative scripts that usually revolve around one or two topics. Practice a lot and hold a dummy performance session in front of your friends and family. Take honest feedback and implement the changes; then record and share on social media. Slowly, once you gain popularity, you can get help from agencies that hold shows by selling tickets.

5. Advertising and Marketing

Their extroverted, creative, and sociable skills make Leos great marketers and advertisers. They can convince people to buy products and can be great at sales. Their chirpy and bright aura will make people believe that they are investing in something worthwhile. You, as a marketer, will, of course, work behind the scenes. However, your creative skills need a push to convince potential buyers to take some form of action. Leos can channel their creativity through persuasion, which is what makes a good marketer great. Leos have the creative ability to create exceptional marketing strategies that work most of the time.

As mentioned earlier, Leos can also specialize in other sub-niches within this discipline, such as social media marketing, salesperson, and product development. Since Leos are open to exploration and want to experience change, they make excellent salespersons. Also, they fit well in any role; whether it's in retail, as a product line manager, or on the business management team, Leos will make sure that they get their share of commission and tips. Their skills benefit any brand and help them increase sales.

6. Orator, Motivational Speaker, or Spokesperson

While this isn't a conventional career choice for all, motivational speaking can be a great choice for Leos. They possess a leadership skill that inspires them to speak in public. When they speak, they portray a sense of authority. Leos are fiery and full of passion, which gives them the fire and motivation that reflects within their speeches. They inspire others to achieve their goals. Even if the speech is a bit weak, Leo's aura and passion will uplift the listener and motivate them to achieve their goals. If you want someone to take charge of a platform and direct others toward success, Leos are your go-to.

This career position is suitable for Leos as motivational speakers, spokespersons, salespersons, publishers, and commodity traders. As a spokesperson, you can either represent your company during interviews or during meetings with venture capitalists. Leos can sell a product or service with ease. They convince people with their charm and sincerity, which also makes them a great fit as marketers and advertisers (more about this in the next section).

7. Makeup Artist or Hair Stylist

The beauty industry is also a great career option for Leos as they love glamor and always try to look their best. Their approach to beauty and glamor is quite serious. They want to look good themselves and want others around them to look their best. They love makeup and exquisite hairstyles. Due to these traits, they can become successful makeup artists and hairstylists. Since Leos have an exquisite taste for distinct hairstyles, they have this natural ability to conceive and cultivate a suitable look for others (whether it's a hairdo or styling their outfits).

Even though Leos are usually indecisive about their own hair, you can count on them to style *your* hair. At the same time, Leos will keep their clients entertained, which will inspire them to return. Other sub-niches and professions within this discipline, also suitable for Leos, are beauty editor, spa owner, and shoot stylist.

8. CEO or Director

As you know, leadership skills are thoroughly ingrained in most Leos; this is why the position of Chief Executive Officer is ideal for Leos. They can motivate and lead a group of employees in any company. This zodiac sign, which the Lion represents, possesses all the qualities required to be a boss. If you are a Leo, you are likely to be chosen for this role. However, make sure that you are ready for it and work hard to make it happen. Being promoted to the position of CEO is not easy. It takes years of hard work, patience, and effort to reach the top. However, since Leos already have the drive and creativity, they merely need to put in the effort and be patient. Also, know that this job is difficult, so be prepared to face unrequited stress.

The same applies to the role of Director. Next, in line with the CEO, the role of a Director is also to lead their group of employees and handle important decisions within the company. As Directors, Leos will extract specific work from their employees and make sure that they are on top of their game. They will get their way by any means and move forward toward just one goal, which is the company's betterment. Also, ordering and bossing around is something that most Directors do, which, as you guessed, is favored by most Leos.

9. Architect or Landscape Designer

Leos are filled with creativity and imagination skills. At the same time, their communication skills are impressive. Collectively, these traits will make them talented architects who can visualize, and design spaces tailored to any client's needs. Architecture also partly involves problem-solving, which Leos are good at. Creating spaces and plans for buildings is something that Leos would love to do, not only to satisfy their creativity but also to impress others. Since architecture is the most visible form of art (imagine drawings being converted into tall buildings that actually exist), they get a solid chance to gain some serious validation. Whether it's an educational facility, a residential building, or a corporate skyscraper, Leos can design it all.

Besides architecture, a similar field is landscape designing. If the Leo has parts of Virgo, Cancer, or Taurus in their horoscopes, this field is the ideal choice for them. Leos appreciate earth and nature, and this discipline lets them explore and experiment with nature. Since Leos are all about attention, it might also show in their work. Their designs for clients are highly likely to garner attention. For instance, their architecture and landscape design might be the loudest, most exquisite, or attention-grabbing on any street. It is less likely to blend within the context unless that is specifically suggested by the client.

10. Lawyer or Judge

Leos are stubborn and will stretch their arguments to prove their point until the other person agrees or gives up. This trait might be well-suited for career positions like a lawyer or a prosecutor. Moreover, Leos respect law and order, a trait rarely found in other signs. Even if they are a beginner in this career, they will climb to the top by showing their talent and using their charm. Their admiration and importance for order and organization are noteworthy, which is also another reason why Leos make successful lawyers and prosecutors. They take pride in fighting for justice and bringing peace to society. It is also a great boost for their egos, which is why they enjoy this career path.

You can also put it this way: a career path that serves law, order, and justice day in and day out might fuel most Leos' narcissistic nature. However, this is not true in all cases. It depends on the opportunity, position, and luck of a Leo. Also, since some Leos do not prefer to argue or are more reserved, this career path can be a bit questionable. However, it has mostly proven to be fit for Leos, so you can consider it if you are a Leo. Their way with words, ability to seduce, and convincing power will make Leos renowned lawyers known to win most cases. Even if the judge is strict, Leo lawyers will twist words and feed their own perceived thoughts to win the case.

11. Writer

Leos also make amazing writers as they love to tell their story and always have a narrative at hand. Their creative skills also enhance their writing style. As writers, Leos need to follow a set of guidelines while having the freedom of creativity, which is a perfect balance for all Leos. As a Leo, if writing fascinates you, try to delve deeper and start your research. Pick a niche – fiction, non-fiction, fantasy, horror; it doesn't matter as long as you are thoroughly invested in it. Try to make the most out of your creative skills and research. As a writer, you will also get a chance to show and sell your work, which will give all Leos the validation they need.

On the other hand, you should also take a look at certain career paths that are not fit for all Leos and should be avoided often as not.

Here are a few of them –

1. Secretary

Leos want to be the boss, and they are worthy too. As you now know, Leos possess excellent leadership skills. They don't like being told what to do. Leos can become great CEOs and bosses, leading the company toward great success through their calculated and wise decisions. Also, people listen to them and not the other way round. They want to apply their mind, which is not quite possible with a secretary's job. They always want to express themselves and despise those who instruct them. With a secretary position, they would feel enclosed and robbed. The feeling of achieving great goals and accomplishing formidable tasks is absent in this position, which is why Leos should probably not consider this position.

2. Retail Worker or Waiter

Even though we mentioned that Leos could work in retail, do not consider this option unless you have no other job positions available. Whether it's retail or waiting on a table, you would absolutely hate the idea of serving others. At times, customers will be rude to you, which is the last thing Leos desires. Their short temperament will make it more difficult for Leos to control the situation, and they will most probably snap back. In retail, most customers want to save money, even if it means letting go of the latest fashion trends. As a Leo, you cannot understand this mindset and hate serving such customers. Leos, who are usually well dressed, will automatically repel frugal people who save money during shopping. While it is not entirely wrong, Leos will never welcome or accept this attitude. If they find a customer who spends as little money as possible, they will stop trying to please them and refrain from giving the best customer support. Assisting is one thing they hate, and they would rather be the one spending money.

As a waiter or waitress, taking orders from customers is also a big no-no for them, especially from the ones with an air of authority around them and that treat others with a lack of respect. Leos would rather be the customer and order their food than be the ones taking orders and serving grumpy customers. If a customer is rude, Leos are most likely to reply with a rude tone, which could cost them their job.

3. Hotel Housekeeper

Again, this position demands Leos be in a lower position with a boss always above them. Being the frontrunners they are, Leos would hate it when the hotel manager comes to check on them every once in a while. Also, if you forget to lock a room or misplace a key, you might get a good bashing. While they already want to be in the top position, this extra bashing and criticizing will make them hate their job even more. Leos can't take criticism well; they are easily offended and refuse to correct their mistakes immediately. If you are in need of some urgent cash, you can take it up as a temporary position, but think twice before you decide to take it up as a permanent job.

Basically, any job that requires Leos to work under someone should be reconsidered by this sign. Unless it is temporary or holds the potential for promotion, rethink your decision before moving ahead.

Where Does the Leo Fit in an Office or Workplace Setting?

Leos love drama, so it's likely to find a Leo near the water cooler or any other popular gossip spot. They judge easily and hate anyone who doesn't think as they do. As you know, it is hard to fight a Leo, and once you do, you might end up in their bad books forever (unless you are their best friend). They will pounce easily and hold their guard. If you are a Leo and have another Leo in the same company, chances are you will become friends and gossip about other employees. However, you will always be in a constant battle for stealing the spotlight.

Some Leos are reserved, which makes up for a very tiny percentage of this zodiac sign. If your workplace has a reserved Leo, they will quietly sit at their desk, minding their business and completing their tasks. However, they will still fish for compliments and want their due credit. Also, it will be difficult for them to handle criticism.

How do Leos Excel at Work?

Even if Leos are hungry for attention and validation, having a Leo on your team is worthwhile. Their strong sense of responsibility, work ethics, and intelligent minds make a solid employee who will reach and fulfill all project goals. A boss usually counts on a Leo to give them ideas regarding their next project, design strategies, and to help other employees move forward. It is highly likely that a Leo will be chosen to lead the next project. Any office team looking for an employee to be the lead speaker in any presentation or conference will always turn to a Leo.

Also, they know their way around fulfilling tasks. Leos are most likely to fulfill a task by finding a smarter route instead of working harder. They will either trick their subordinates into completing a task or find a simpler solution by racking their brains. And being the group leader, they will put the best minds on the project to increase the success rates.

All in all, creativity, a strong sense of responsibility, work ethics, and smart working techniques make a Leo a valuable employee. However, beware of their presence around you as they could easily steal your spot and are more likely to get the promotion. Even if you show a better performance, they will charm and influence your boss, which will automatically make them a better choice. Lastly, Leos are extremely loyal, which means that you can trust them with their decisions, and they will never cheat.

If all goes well, your company will be blessed with a deserving Leo as your boss, who is courageous, intelligent, and responsible.

These reasons also explain why Leos make great businessmen. They portray an authoritative tone, which most entrepreneurs should possess. They demand what they want and are not afraid to speak up. If they see anything wrong happening in the company, they will immediately redirect their stance and make sure that all employees are at the top of their game. Their ambitious drive is infectious, and they display a massive amount of strength and stamina to fulfill their goals. If you have a Leo for your boss, they will accurately gauge your worth. While they need attention, they will reciprocate a similar amount of appreciation and attention to their employees who perform well under their leadership.

Also, since Leos are open to risks, they are most likely to open a business and succeed rather than work as an employee and take instructions from someone else.

Obstacles a Leo Might Experience at Work

Now that you know the career paths that you can tap into, let's take a look at the negative traits of a Leo at work and how those could affect their work and productivity.

1. They are Impulsive, Which Can Lead to Bad Decisions

Most Leos are impulsive, which can lead to some repercussions, especially of the emotional sort. Even though Leos are quick with decision making, an impulsive nature can drive them to take ill-advised actions.

2. They Might Feel Snubbed at Times

A Leo likes and wants their share of validation when they fulfill a project. If the boss doesn't appreciate their work, they might feel low or even angry. They want their share of credit and others to appreciate their valuable presence in a team, especially if they have helped to sign a lucrative deal. Whether it's a big project they handled or maintaining a small winning streak in the workplace, they will want appreciation for all instances. If it's an important overseas project, be ready to praise your Leo subordinate as they will need the extra credit during such significant instances. While Leo bosses do praise their employees for their efforts, extremely self-centered Leo bosses will take all the credit. Even though it is less likely, you can expect this to happen.

3. Leos Can Suffer from Occasional Spells of Laziness

This is mainly due to getting bored and distracted. While Leos do have a strong sense of responsibility, they are often distracted, and this results in laziness and procrastination, which is unacceptable in a work setting. Whenever they feel lazy, they find a way to get things done with less effort or give it to their team members. Surprisingly, even when they are lazy, they get things done on time.

4. The Workplace Can be a Bit Melodramatic

You already know how Leos love drama. They are dramatic in their personal life and tend to show it when they are a bit overworked or don't get their share of attention. They are either too snubbed or will create havoc in the workplace. With Leos around, you will occasionally face tense situations due to some aspect of their nature.

Tips for the Leo to Achieve a Fulfilling Work-Life

Learning and being aware of your negative traits is half the battle won. To win it all, you must work on your weaknesses and navigate them to achieve success in your work life.

1. Set a Routine

Even though Leos have a strong sense of responsibility, they can, at times, be too lazy and distracted due to their impulsive nature. If you are a Leo, you will find yourself daydreaming about the next big purchase on your work desk, which will ruin your daily goal plan. To save yourself from being distracted, you must set a routine. Plan your day by making a list of your tasks; this will not only help you stay on track, but you will also fulfill your tasks sooner.

2. Work on Your Communication Skills and Techniques

If your ultimate goal is to be the CEO of your company, you must work on your communication skills. While smooth-talking is a part of a Leo's charm, being a boss might require a more authoritative yet calmer tone, one that your employees will listen to and follow. Practice your communication skills by engaging with other people, listening to others, taking time to respond, and simplifying the message. It is also necessary to make eye contact and work on your body language while communicating with others, especially if the other person is a significant figure within your discipline.

Also, Leos can be a bit arrogant, which is quite apparent in their tone. Even if they don't mean to offend someone, their tone can give them away. This is why Leos should work on their communication skills; it will help them climb the corporate ladder rapidly and help Leos control their egos.

3. Prepare or Discover Your Creative Outlet

Your creative outlet is telling yourself that you need some "me" time. When you are always busy and unable to take time out for yourself, you become exhausted and delay your goals. Everyone needs a break. Finding your creative outlet will keep you enthusiastic in all areas of your life and help you combat distractions and procrastination. Whether it's a karaoke night or a DIY project, your creative outlet will help you develop new skills while you enjoy your break time. Finding and pursuing your creative outlet is necessary to keep your mental health in check and give you your well-deserved break.

If something is not letting you sleep at night, it could be your creative outlet. Pay close attention and acknowledge the idea. Is there a thought nagging you all the time and depriving you of sleep? Does your house need re-modeling? Are you stuck with a business idea? What is it? Reflect on your thoughts and work toward them. Another way to find your creative outlet is to find a creative studio in your locality. It can be an art studio, a music arena, or a book reading club. Dig deeper and find a space that calls out to you.

4. Find Your Inspiration

This is related to what you learned above. Your inspiration will help you maintain the drive and keep you motivated. Do you want to start a new business? Have you always dreamed of authoring a book? Are you looking forward to changing your career? Take the step and stay inspired. Even though Leos are motivated and motivate others, they might feel stuck at some point, which is when finding one's inspiration helps. Even if you don't have a recurring thought or a plan, try new things and find a new passion. Join an acting class, take up baking, open your candle business; take the leap, and do what makes you happy. Leos are bright and creative individuals and finding their inspiration and passion will always keep them on their feet.

To sum up, Leos at work are usually reliable and commit their mind and soul to achieve their goals. At times, they can be distracted by laziness, and their impulsive nature can get in their way. Once Leos apply the tricks mentioned above, they will climb the corporate ladder quickly and fight their way to taking over leadership. They make excellent bosses and CEOs, and they have a knack for conducting smooth business. Give the required attention and credit to Leos in the workplace, or you will have an easier time calming them down.

Chapter 7: What does the Leo Need?

In this chapter, we will discuss some effective ways for the Leo to maximize and make the most of their traits and to navigate the tougher parts of their sign. Even though we discussed the important traits, strengths, weaknesses, and how to navigate them, let's discuss some quick tips to summarize these methods and help the Leo take better control of their lives. These tips are simple to apply in the Leos' everyday life and create the highest impact.

As You Learned, a Leo Would Need the Following

Attention and Spotlight: As you clearly know by now, a Leo wants their share of attention and spotlight. They cannot bear it when someone else takes the center stage.

Respect: The attention they get should be genuine. They can easily spot fake gestures and will automatically push away from them. With a Leo, give respect to earn respect.

Passionate Love: Leos are extremely passionate and want equal love in return. Whether it's a romantic relationship or a one-time sexual encounter, they will please their partners with a burning passion.

True Friendship: Leos make friends easily but take some time before they get close to someone. They expect loyalty, trust, constant support, and respect in a friendship, which makes for true friendship.

Luxury: Leos want everything luxurious and expensive. They give expensive gifts and want the same in return. Give some cash to a Leo, and you will find it being wasted on an unnecessary luxurious item.

These are the basic necessities that a Leo wants in all areas of their life.

Quick Tips for Leos

1. Polish your Personality or Image

While you are already working on building your personality every day and trying to be the best version of you, Leos should focus on creating their identity and discovering a unique trait. It will help you polish your image and help you to stand apart from the crowd. Since you like attention, this quick tip will help you regain the center stage. Make sure that you are building an image that reflects self-promotion. For instance, if you are building a new business or designing a new logo for your brand, this unique aspect of your personality should reflect in other aspects of your life, too. It will further polish your image and help your brand stand apart.

Whether it's your email address, brand logo, or business card, the things you use and design should reflect you. Add the colors you like and the ones that represent your aura. Even though it is a long shot, this tip will help you get more recognition in the professional world and push your business toward success. Your face represents your brand and vice versa. So, it is necessary to make a good impression, part of which comes to you naturally as a Leo.

2. Eat More Sun-Ripened Foods

The food you eat directly affects your physical and mental health. Leos are advised to consume sun-ripened foods, and local organic is best. Since the Sun sign governs Leos, sun-ripened foods will keep you close to nature and make you more radiant. Sun-ripened food is also known to make a Leo feel good, healthier, and more energetic. These foods include sun-dried tomatoes, grapes, apricots, chilies, hot peppers, and dates.

Sun-dried harvest is usually free of chemicals, harmful pesticides, and is extremely healthy. Sun-drying fruits and veggies increases the shelf life and helps to keep health benefits intact; the best part about sun-dried food is that it retains all nutrients and can be used for a prolonged period. Have a few sundried foods daily to improve health and look more radiant. Even though eating sun-dried food should be a priority, try not to miss out on the occasional indulgences to retain your sanity, too. Have that slice of cake or a piece of chocolate that you have been craving.

3. Smile and Laugh More Often

Naturally, smiling and laughing more often will make you look more radiant, brighter, and attract people to you. People are attracted to those who have a positive aura, which is often seen in people who are always happy. Even though Leos seem bright and radiant, smiling and laughing more often will boost your immune system and enhance your heart health. You worry less, which reduces stress and improves mental health. Also, the more you smile and laugh, the better people you will be attracting to you. It will help you develop better connections in your personal life and attract opportunities in the professional world.

Try to take time out and meet your close friends often. Plan outings or invite them to play board games. Try more activities that make you happy. Watch comedy shows or stand-up acts. Along with that, play with your kids or your younger cousins to unleash your inner child. Lastly, attend fun outdoor events such as concerts, amusement park trips, or even a day at the beach to feel happy and obtain inner peace.

4. Take Care of Your Physical and Mental Health

While this applies to all signs, Leos must particularly focus on their physical and mental health as this sign is usually proactive and expends its energy aimlessly. Eat right, exercise at least thirty minutes every day, and drink a lot of water. Pay attention to your diet and try to add as many nutrients as possible; this will improve your physical health and stamina, and help you lose or maintain weight. Besides this, you should also practice mental health improvement exercises such as meditation and yoga. Improve your sleep pattern and get seven-to-eight hours of sleep every night.

Besides your mental and physical health, you must also focus on your spiritual and emotional health. Take care of your heart and give it the proper time to heal and develop, especially if there has been a traumatic situation. It will also help Leo men express their feelings, as they are the ones who hold back. Have a heart-to-heart conversation with your loved ones, practice chakra yoga to open your body's chakras, and practice self-healing. Focus on exercises that open your heart chakra.

5. Add More Warm Colors to Your Color Palette

The Sun sign that rules Leos make the individuals of this zodiac sign seem warm and bright. The bright colors of the sun should also be adopted by all Leos and added to their color palette. Hues like red, orange, and yellow should be a regular part of your color palette. The things you wear, use, and eat should include these colors in some form. These bright colors will enhance your personality and make you more attractive. Your liveliness and playful spirit need just a touch of these colors on and around you.

If you still prefer to stick to darker shades, add some bright accessories, such as a belt or a hat with a yellow or orange touch. These colors also reflect the fire element and the burning passion within most Leos. Do not be shy about wearing a warm-colored outfit with a dash of bold red lipstick. As a Leo, you are likely to carry this look with confidence and make a bold statement. Apart from outfits and accessories, add warm shades in accents of the things around you, such as your rug, sofa, curtains, towels, etc.

Quick Tips for the Friends of Leos

1. Let Them Have the Center Stage

Even though we mentioned this tip earlier, emphasizing it is crucial. Since Leos live for attention, they will despise being friends with someone who will take the spotlight. If you value your Leo friend, let them have their share of attention and enjoy their moment. Whether it's a karaoke night or a birthday party, let them be in the spotlight. Even if you don't prefer to share the spotlight, try to be cooperative and support your Leo friend's wants. If you want to go an extra length, encourage and hype your friend by telling one of their funniest stories to the crowd or complimenting them in front of everyone.

These sly techniques are a way to win your Leo friend's heart and stay close friends in the long run. Since Leos like to be validated, they will automatically feel more valuable and closer to you; this is particularly helpful for those Leos who are shy and more reserved. They want to be validated but are unable to garner attention. As their friend, take the initiative and help them experience the attention they often crave. Basically, let them shine.

2. Never Try to Take Advantage of their Situation

As you know, Leos are extremely loyal and trustworthy, and they expect the same in return. Their generous and loyal trait can make them seem unreasonably kind, which some people mistake for being naïve. If you claim to be their best or close friend, you will never take advantage of their generosity and kindness. Once Leos figure out your true intentions are not in their best interests, they will lose respect and the trust invested in you. While it is easier for them to forgive you, it will be difficult for them to forget. Do not exploit their liberality, knowingly or unknowingly.

Do not try to reap the benefits of their cooperative attitude. It will take them no time to reciprocate harshly. You will notice them unleashing their wrath and bringing their inner Lion out. Do not trigger Leos by breaking their trust in any way. Try your best not to make them angry.

3. Be Good Listeners

When Leos are hurt or are in pain, their hearts are heavy, and they want someone to listen to them. As a friend of a Leo, they might turn to you at times. Let them vent and feel lighter. Do not listen to give advice; only listen to what they say, which makes you a good listener. Even though it might seem a bit unpleasant or repetitive, sit through it because that is what best friends do. If they can trust you listening to them during unpleasant situations, they will try to maintain the friendship and be drawn to you with the passing of time.

When they vent, Leos generally let out all their anger and frustration, which is enough to make them smile. After calming down, they develop an ability to think rationally. Don't interrupt them when they are venting. Let them blurt it all out and express their deepest regrets in front of you. To calm them down, try to comfort them by being empathetic.

For instance, if your Leo friend says, "I was trying to call you for two hours as I wanted someone to talk to me and you were unavailable," you should reply, "I understand that you needed me during those intense hours, and I should have been there for you. I can understand that it must be frustrating."

Apart from these tips, you should shower your Leo friend with presents, compliments, and flatter them as much as you can. Try to be sincere about your feelings as Leos can easily spot it if you are fake.

Conclusion

To sum up, let's describe the personality traits of Leos in three words - vivacious, passionate, and theatrical. A Leo is like a lion in the savannah - the powerful king. Leos are powerful lions in the concrete jungle who try to pave their own paths and emerge victoriously. They know how to take the spotlight, are always curious, extremely creative, and born leaders.

Leos at home, work, and social gatherings are almost the same - they are curious about everything and always ready to try new skills. And their supreme talent and leadership skills are impeccable and a hit with others.

If you are a Leo, try to align your weaknesses and strengths in the right direction to achieve your goals and create the best version of yourself. Work on your stubbornness and vanity. At the same time, take proper advantage of your strengths.

If you are a friend, parent, or partner of a Leo, you must pay a lot of attention to them and handle intense situations with ease. Show them affection and let them have their center stage in public settings. If you are trying to impress, seduce, or date a Leo, dress nicely, give expensive presents, and compliment them often. Make them feel wanted and important.

As a Leo, this information will not only give you better control over your life and relevant dimensions of it, but you will also be able to change your life significantly. If applied correctly, this book's advice will help you excel at work, with your relationships, and at social events, which will ultimately build your confidence and help you succeed in life.

It is now time to put this information, tips, and advice into action and win the world. Good luck!

Here's another book by Mari Silva that you might like

Your Free Gift (only available for a limited time)

Thanks for getting this book! If you want to learn more about various spirituality topics, then join Mari Silva's community and get a free guided meditation MP3 for awakening your third eye. This guided meditation mp3 is designed to open and strengthen ones third eye so you can experience a higher state of consciousness. Simply visit the link below the image to get started.

https://spiritualityspot.com/meditation

References

Astrologer, M. H. M. H. and Reader, T., & Hall, author of "Astrology: A. C. I. G. to the Z. " our editorial process M. (n.d.). *12 Tips for When the Sun Is in Leo.* LiveAbout. Retrieved from https://www.liveabout.com/tips-when-the-sun-in-leo-206836

Astrologer, P. L. C. H. (n.d.). *How a Leo-Virgo Cusp Sign Handles Life & Love.* Retrieved from https://horoscopes.lovetoknow.com/astrology-signs-personality/leo-cusp-traits

Astrology King. (n.d.). Astrology King. Retrieved from http://astrologyking.com/

Best Careers & Worst Jobs For Leo Zodiac Signs, Per Astrology. (2020, March 22). Your Tango. https://www.yourtango.com/2020332362/best-careers-worst-jobs-all-leo-zodiac-signs-astrology

Blog. (n.d.). The Dark Pixie Astrology. Retrieved from http://www.thedarkpixieastrology.com/blog

Damian, A. (2020, June 24). *AMAZING: Your 4 Dream Jobs if You Are a Leo.* Themagichoroscope.com. https://themagichoroscope.com/zodiac/best-jobs-leo

Find the Best Career for Your Zodiac Sign - Leo | ZipRecruiter®. (2019, May 7). ZipRecruiter. https://www.ziprecruiter.com/blog/best-career-paths-leo/

http://leohoroscope.in/. (n.d.). Retrieved from http://leohoroscope.in/

https://www.facebook.com/ZodiacFire. (2018, November 14). *21 Secrets Of The Leo Personality...* Zodiac Fire. https://zodiacfire.com/leo-personality/

Leo Friendship Compatibility: Be Patient! (n.d.). Tarot.com. Retrieved from https://www.tarot.com/astrology/compatibility/friends/leo

Leo Parent, Leo Child. (n.d.). *Baby Centre UK*. Retrieved from https://www.babycentre.co.uk/h1029981/leo-parent-leo-child

Mom365. (2020). *8 Things to Know About Your Leo Child*. Mom365.com. https://www.mom365.com/mom/astrology/all-about-your-leo-childs-astrology

My Leo Zodiac Sign: Friendship. (n.d.). Www.Horoscope.com. https://www.horoscope.com/zodiac-signs/leo/friendship

On the Cusp: What being a mix of Big Leo Energy and Virgo perfectionism means for your personality. (2019, August 20). Well+Good. https://www.wellandgood.com/leo-virgo-cusp/

Power of Positivity. (2016, August 3). *7 Things You Need To Know If You're Friends With a Leo*. Power of Positivity: Positive Thinking & Attitude. https://www.powerofpositivity.com/7-things-need-know-youre-friends-leo/

Rae, L. (n.d.). *7 Reasons Why You Should Do Business With A Leo*. Elite Daily. https://www.elitedaily.com/life/do-business-with-leos/1144979

Register, J., & Godio, M. (2020, May 7). *Your Zodiac Sign's Biggest Problem and How to Fix It*. Cosmopolitan. https://www.cosmopolitan.com/sex-love/a23490075/zodiac-sign-personality-traits-flaw/

The Leo Child: Leo Girl & Boy Traits & Personality | Zodiac Signs for Kids. (n.d.). Www.Buildingbeautifulsouls.com. Retrieved from https://www.buildingbeautifulsouls.com/zodiac-signs/zodiac-signs-kids/leo-child-traits-characteristics-personality/

The Leo Employee - Personality and Characteristics | Futurescopes. (n.d.). Futurescopes.com. Retrieved from https://futurescopes.com/astrology/leo/2767/leo-employee-personality-and-characteristics

These 10 Fascinating, Fiery Facts Will Tell You So Much About Your Leo Baby. (n.d.). Romper. Retrieved from https://www.romper.com/p/10-fascinating-facts-about-leo-babies-the-most-fiery-fire-sign-of-them-all-18366362

(2020). Theastrocodex.com. http://theastrocodex.com

Made in the USA
Middletown, DE
03 September 2021